ON OIL PAINTING

WITH A CHAPTER ON TEMPERA

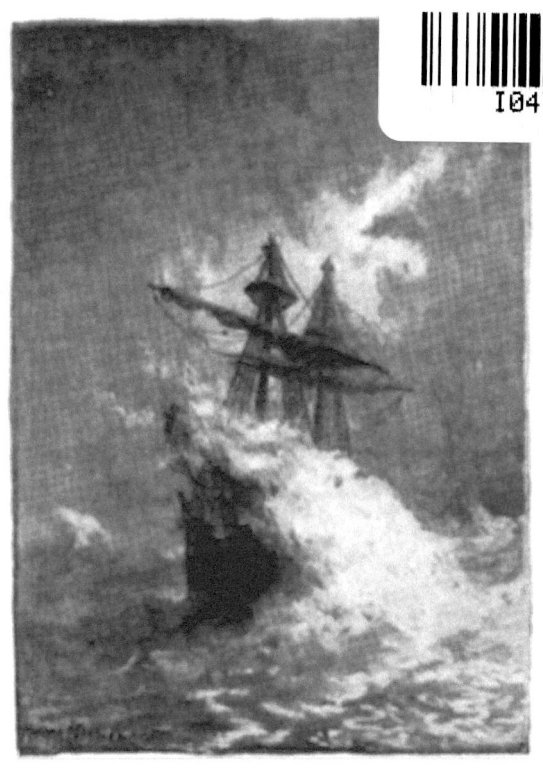

BY

HUME NISBET

Author of " Painting in Water Colour "

ELEVENTH EDITION

B

British Library Cataloguing-in-Publication Data
A catalogue record for this book is available from
the British Library

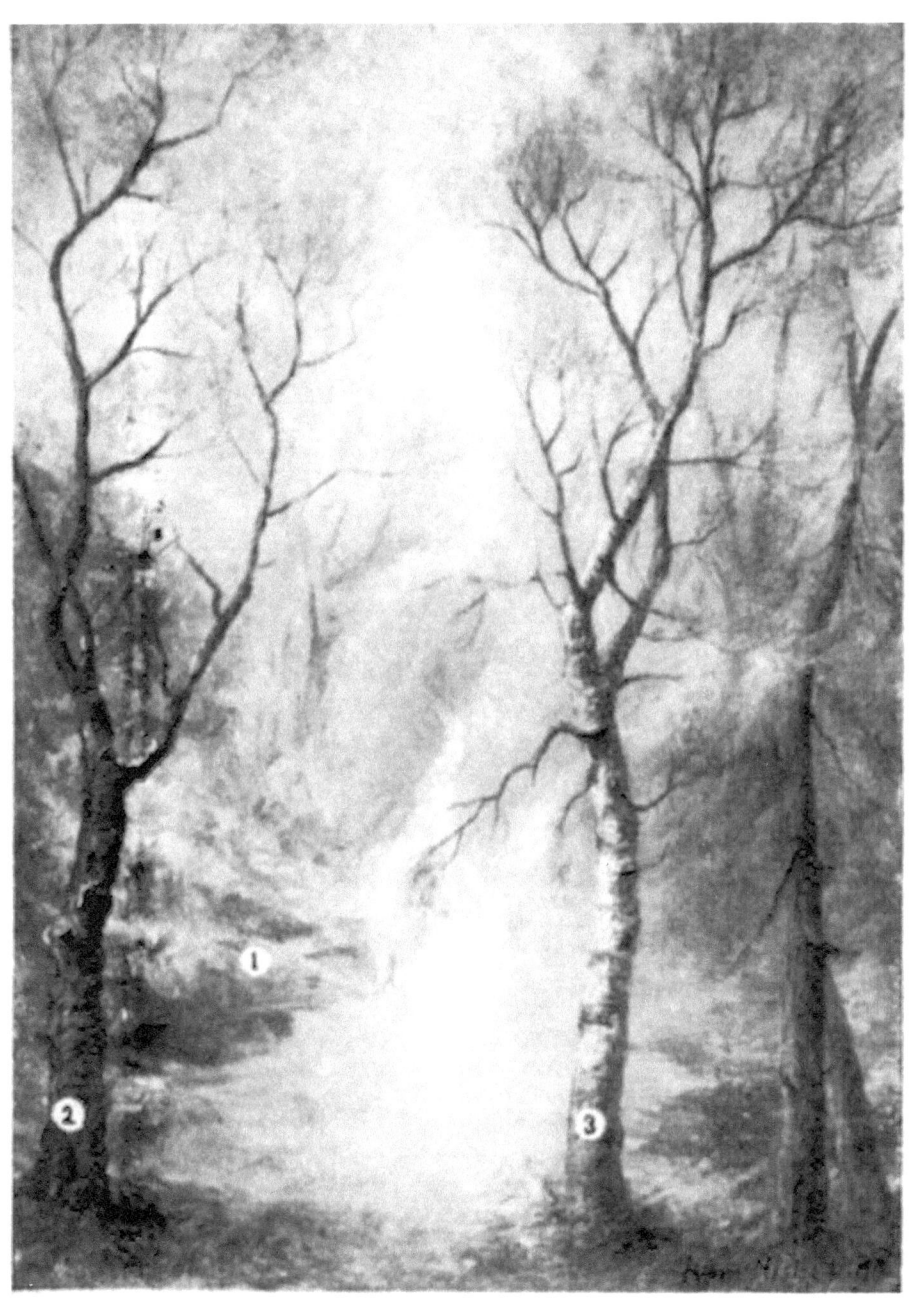

FRONTISPIECE.—Spring Study in three stages.

CONTENTS.

———◆———

ILLUSTRATIONS.

———◆———

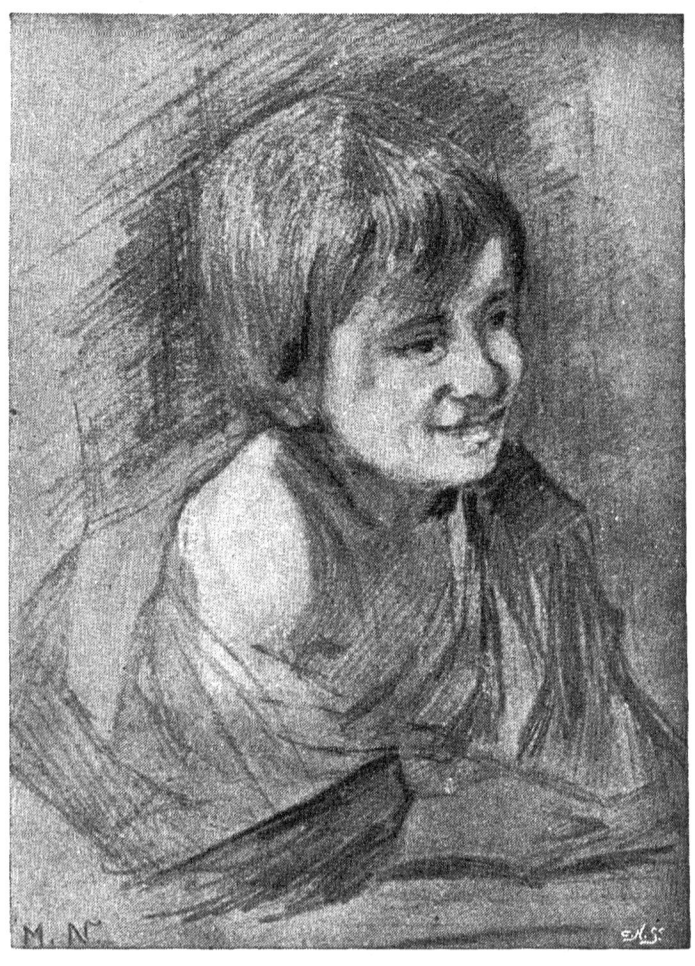

Study after Murillo, from a pencil
drawing by Martin North.

ON OIL PAINTING.

CHAPTER I.

HOW TO APPROACH THE SUBJECT.

I SUPPOSE that, before the desire comes over my readers to take up a book with the above title upon its cover, they know something about the rudiments of Art. As children you have doubtless coloured prints and drawn strange and quaint likenesses of the people and animals you saw close to you, yet I do not think that one out of twenty of the children who are fond of drawing began his career by trying to undertake a tree or a tea-cup. Men, women, horses, cows, dogs and cats were the subjects which first woke to action the latent art instincts. The tree and the tea-cup are advanced and acquired tastes.

The child of civilization resembles in this the savage and primitive artist. The savage cuts the image of the snake upon his spear, the civilized child, as yet untaught, tries to reproduce the domesticated cat upon his slate. He goes to school, and amongst other branches of education he gets cottages and windmills to copy and shade, with a head now and again, which when he has done them do not look unlike those much valued creations of the early masters which can be seen in the National and other Galleries. I expect, from their productions, that these Masters were, like the savage and the untutored child, self-taught geniuses.

I am supposing that the student has got beyond shaded heads and impossible cottages. He has been taught to modify his ambition and mortify his spirit with the rigid practice of straight and curved lines, the pot-hooks of art. I do not expect him to draw a circle with the same accuracy as a pair of compasses can, or put the spot in the exact centre, for these are tricks of legerdemain which very few professional artists would attempt, although by long and constant practice the most commonplace and mechanical hand might attain to this flimsy perfection.

Yet I do hope that, before you attempt to purchase the materials which I shall presently describe. you are able to draw decently straight horizontal and perpendicular lines, and also make a free and sweeping curve with your pencil, your chalk and your charcoal. If you can do these feats intelligently, you will be able, with a little practice, careful consideration, and severe self-criticism, to draw whatever is placed before you. When you have reached this stage then you may indulge in paints and brushes, *but not before.*

To reach this stage you must proceed by degrees and not attempt too much at the start. A tea-cup, a round ball, and a square block of wood, are the best objects to test your powers of straight and curved line drawing, for these three objects hold the same difficulties as the most intricate ornament, pattern, design, and form throughout the works of Nature, or the craft of Man.

The trouble which will perpetually beset you is the intricacy and combination of lines and curves, that is, the details of the subjects you may have decided to copy, which are so apt to confuse your mind and disturb your sense of proportion. To get over this, you must constantly think upon your cup, your ball, and your square block ; and try, for a time, to forget that your subject may be a human being, an animal, or a landscape. Steady your mind as you watch it carefully, and consider it only as a combination of lines and curves, with certain spaces between each different curve and line. If you do this you will be surprised how quickly it all comes within your range of grip and knowledge.

These spaces and proportions are the first points which you have to consider—the relation of one part to another. Your glance takes in a certain range. That is your picture, study it in a general way with its masses and leading points, and, when you have grasped these definitely, jot them in with dots or light touches with your pencil or charcoal Measure these dots, one from the other, and, when you are satisfied that they occupy their correct places, proceed to fix upon the central or most important of these points and draw that lightly and roughly to the size you think it ought to take on your paper or canvas.

This done, draw and measure your next important point, using as your gauge the object you have first sketched in, and measure the others from it. In this manner, what might have confused you if you had started at random, becomes delightfully easy and simple.

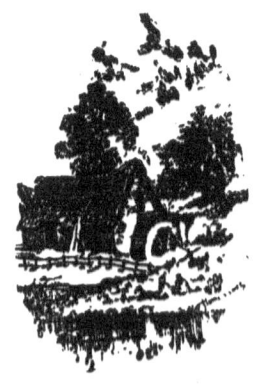

CHAPTER II.

ON GENERAL DRAWING AND PLANNING OUT.

As to the correct system of learning to draw, there is, and must ever be, a diversity of opinion, as there has been and ever will be respecting the proper mode of painting.

Many great painters have been almost self-taught ; in such instances the organs of form and size were so largely developed, also the sense of observation so keen, that accuracy was an instinct rather than an accomplishment, so that any object out of drawing, or lacking in proportion, would produce the same discord to their ocular nerves as a false note would to the ear of a born musician. Many persons who are unable to draw themselves, or at least have no taste for such work, are possessed of this same innate faculty, and make good critics and fault-finders as far as outline and form are concerned.

In painting also, the qualities which go to form a colourist are instinctive and nature-born as decidedly as the true musician and poet must be gifted by Nature. It is a singular fact, however, that the Artist who is instinctively a colourist, of the purest and highest order, is often defective in form. When however both form and colour unite, very little training is required to finish this genius which Nature has already formed.

Yet, to be able to compete with success in this highly cultured age, a certain amount of strict training is absolutely necessary, even for the amateur, while the heaven-made genius never yet was gifted enough to be able to do without some instruction.

Of course, after he has overcome the rudiments and learnt a few of the necessary *tricks* and secrets of his art, he may train himself, while every work he projects and carries out will be a study and a progressive step on his long road towards perfection. Indeed this is the only true method of regarding art ; each fresh picture or study is another problem to be discovered and mastered, and this you will find out for yourself as you work and strive ; otherwise you will sink into the slough of the self-satisfied 'pot-boilers,' whose qualified successes are infinitely worse than progressive failures.

The greatest genius must learn how to measure his subject and so test the accuracy of his eye. He must be taught how to hold his charcoal pencil or brush so as to measure the different parts of his figures or landscapes, for Nature

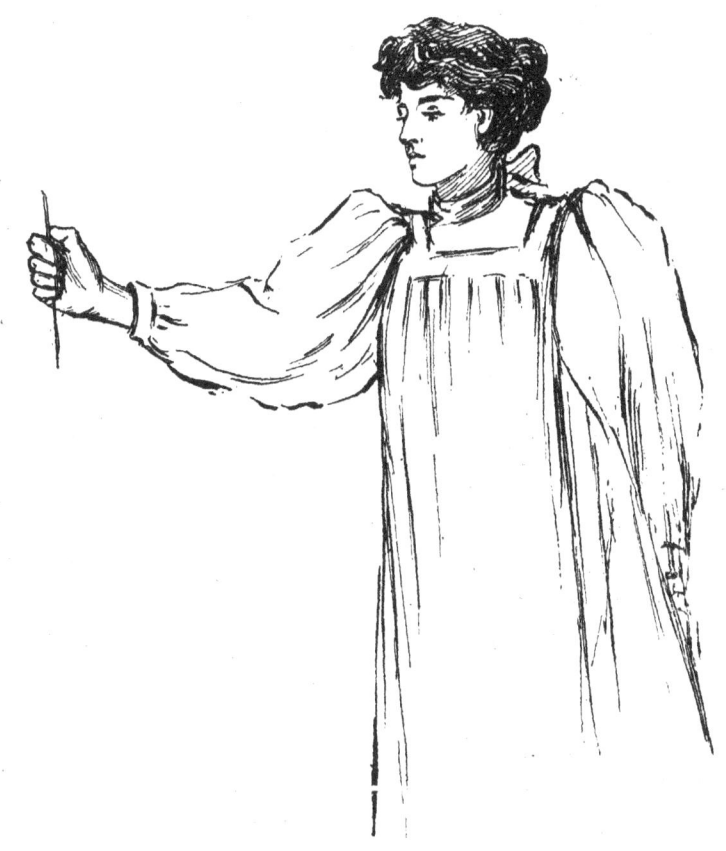

Plate 1.

Measuring the Subject.

stops short at this part of her gift, although she may have given him a very true eye for just proportions. When he can measure his subject properly, then he is in the position to contest with his critics.

This is the proper method of measuring : grip your pencil, charcoal-stick or brush-handle with your four fingers, allowing it to stand upright far enough to be able to use your thumb as a mark, as in Illustration Fig. 1.

Stretch your arm out stiffly to the elbow, holding the upper part of the arm from the shoulder quite steady, and moving the lower part from the elbow, up and down, as required. Shut one eye, and place your pencil or measuring stick between your open eye and the object ; take one portion, for instance, if it is a figure, for the first measurement ; take the head as your gauge of comparison, with your thumb-nail as the mark of your measuring stick ; move your hand from the elbow only, and from the head to the feet, noting the portion of the figure that each head length reaches to ; do the same with the breadth of the figure, with the head always as your gauge. Other parts of the picture you can measure in a larger way, say for instance, the figure, half or quarter figure, as the space may be which you desire to test (I speak here where objects are drawn from the life, or from a distance). In more detailed measurement you will take a nose length as your gauge, or half a nose length, if you wish to be particular. Only take care and do not move your upper arm, or *humerus*, otherwise you cannot depend upon the accuracy of your measurement. A little practice is required to be able to do this properly. In landscapes, you measure in the same way ; take a distant steeple, or tree, and measure all the other portions of the scene from this selected part.

I have told you how to plan out your picture first, so as to get objects in their places, by dots. If it is a figure subject, you will begin by drawing a perpendicular line through the middle of each figure, *i.e.*, according to their positions ; if leaning, or reclining, then they may be slanting or horizontal lines. Across this centre line, draw horizontal lines for each head-length ; then in the face draw lines representing nose-lengths ; then begin to block in, *i.e.*, draw roughly and as squarely as you can, the outline. Think about your first block of wood study at this stage and forget your curves. Draw your figure out like that square block of wood, leaving yourself plenty of room to cut away and refine afterwards. Think only upon your rugged proportions at this stage, and never mind such details as neck, waist, hands, feet or features (*see* Plate 2).

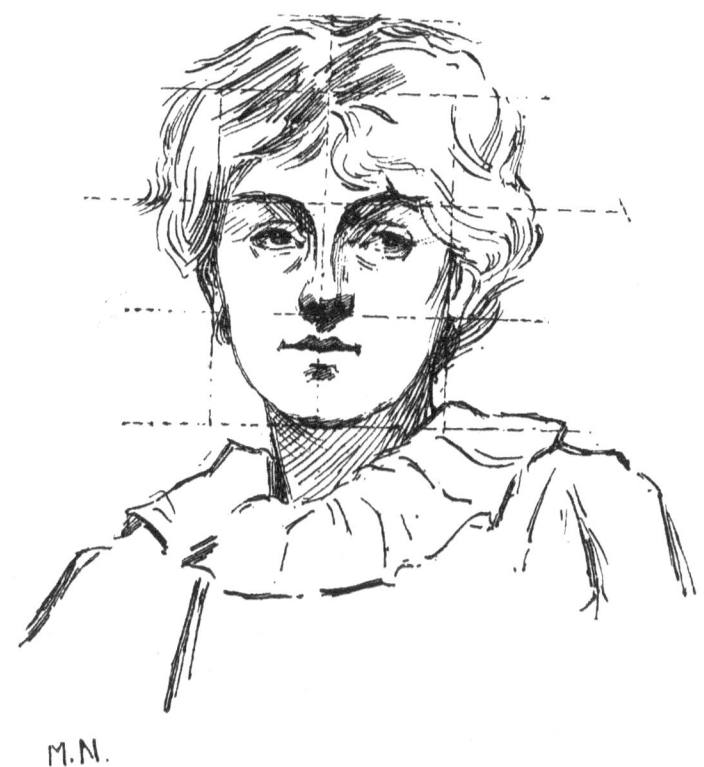

M.N.

Plate 2.

A head divided into nose lengths.

Landscapes you will treat in the same manner, also ornaments, flowers, and drapery or accessories. A house, steeple, or castle, draw in like square blocks. Trees box in squarely with the main limbs and trunks passing through the centre and all the smaller branches disregarded. Mountains, fields and rivers, or lakes—draw only their angles, and positions, with the more massive clouds.

Second Stage. Begin by studying and measuring, as well as watching keenly the relative positions of one object with another. See against what part of the body, say, the hands rest or touch. What position the figure and its individual parts occupy as regards other objects, animate or inanimate, and draw guiding lines from the one portion to the other. By-and-bye, when you are more accomplished, you will be able to do with imaginary lines, but meantime stick to definite lines, they are easy to obliterate when no longer needed, and still regard your subject as a rough block of wood or stone.

Be most particular and accurate over this stage in your work, for if you get right now, you will have nothing to trouble your mind as to the drawing when you come to the painting, but if you make a mistake here, your troubles and anxieties will be endless afterwards, every critic who finds fault will unsettle you, until you fall into numberless blunders trying to correct, and end in spoiling everything. Be positive in your own mind that your drawing is correct, for on that point you can make yourself positive now, or never, and if correct you may work with confidence and defy criticism.

Above all things, do not for a single instant relax your vigilance of what you actually see of the masses, and put nothing in that you cannot see, because you may know it to be there. A man has two legs, but you only see one, without the slightest sign of the other. Stick to that single limb and leave the other to take care of itself.

The same advice relates to landscape and everything that can be reproduced. Never move from your first standpoint under any temptation, and never try the impossible artistic feat of looking behind a wall or a tree. If you adhere to these instructions of drawing only what is before you, in their exact position towards each other, with the straight and slanting lines at the angles they appear to you, whether you understand the laws which govern perspective or not you can hardly make a mistake.

The rules of perspective, with the exception of interiors and architectural subjects purely, are not at all difficult to understand.

Where you stand or sit, is your stand-point or bottom line of your picture, or, to speak more exactly, you are outside your picture, so that your stand-point is below your canvas at any distance you like to determine.

Directly opposite you lies your point of sight. It all depends where you are looking, whether it is in the centre of the canvas, or on one side of it, only remember, that you have to look up at objects above your point of sight, so that you cannot look into them.

From the root of your nose between the eyes is one point from which lines of vision diverge from side to side of the landscape or interior ; therefore as your canvas represents the same area that your vision takes in, the imaginary rays from your eyes cover the space of your canvas. A straight line runs from your eyes to the point of sight, while other lines diverge in a circle all ronud.

From the point of sight, *i.e.*, the farthest point in the scene before you, lines of rays diverge and spread over the scene and canvas ; a perpendicular line from top to bottom crosses the point of sight as you may see the rays from the setting or rising sun ; the centre one straight up and down, the others slanting by degrees. Across the point of sight, a straight horizontal line passes from side to side of the scene and canvas, as the perpendicular line passes from top to bottom, forming an exact St. Andrew's

cross. All diverging or slanting lines below this
'*horizontal line*' are looked into. All diverging
lines above it are looked up at.

The horizontal line marks your extreme
distance. Whatever lies below it must slant
downwards, *i.e.*, the bottom lines of walls, windows,
streets, floors, &c. Whatever lies above it must
slant in the different degrees, from the point of
sight upwards and away, *i.e.*, the tops of houses,
ceilings, &c. These are the main laws of
perspective, when objects are placed within these
direct lines.

Sometimes however a chair, table, house or
other object may be placed at an angle so that
you are able to see both sides, one receding
toward the point of sight and the other towards
some point away from your canvas. The point of
sight does not govern this other side, but the
horizontal line must do so always ; at least, in most
cases it must govern every object. I shall tell you
afterwards where it does not.

To meet this difficulty of the angle :—Take one
of the slanting lines (suppose it to be the top of a
table or the side of a street) follow its course until
it crosses the horizontal line, and you have here
what is termed the *point of distance.*

Probably that point may lie beyond the
extreme side of your canvas. Carry in imagination

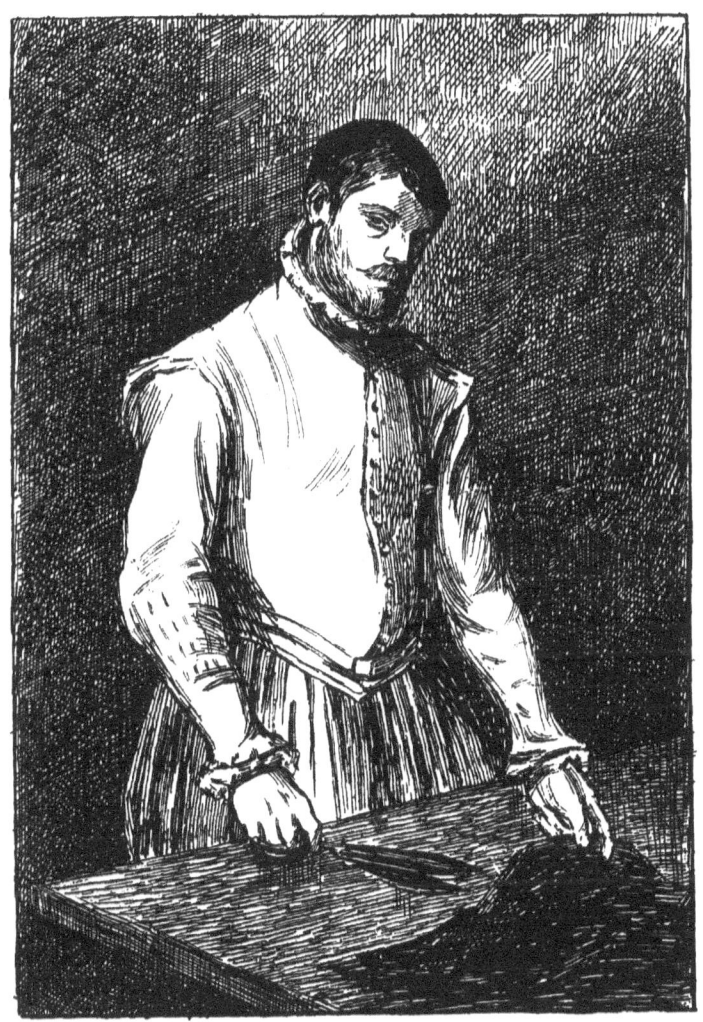

Plate 3.

Study after Moroni from a pen
drawing by Martin North

your horizontal line to where the slanting line which you have fixed upon as your gauge, meets and crosses it, and let that determine all the other slanting lines from this side; those which are below it will be more acute, those above that test slanting line more obtuse. This is the principle which governs angular perspective.

The exceptions to these rules are with some intricate staircases or ceilings, or where buildings are placed in an eccentric position on a sloping terrace or a hill-side. In such cases, it will be necessary for you to take liberties and make false horizontal lines to meet the case in point, and in the majority of these your own eyes with some slanting line must be your guides out of the difficulty. Of course, if it is an architectural drawing or plan you are making, then it will be necessary for you to study the more exact and scientific rules of architectural perspective; but, as this branch lies outside my present subject, I shall not touch upon it more closely, as I want to teach you only how to paint pictures in oil, and not to make architects of you.

You have now mapped out and measured your drawing in all its larger parts, and if you are satisfied as to its correctness and solidity, we will now proceed to the

Third Stage. This is the stage where your

curve drawing comes in ; yet, even here, I strongly advise you to draw still as squarely and largely as you can. Get your outlines in, more particularly with the different prominences and depressions, also such details as the eyes, nose, mouth, breasts, hair, principal muscles, and larger details. In landscape you can put in your different markings for windows, doors, also getting the shape of the trees with their characters.

I have not yet mentioned, that all this preliminary work you have been sketching in with charcoal, which, being easily rubbed or dusted off the canvas, will enable you to make what corrections are needful as you go along. Now if you are satisfied that you can do no more with that material, I would advise you to go over your work with a black-lead pencil, re-forming your outlines as you make them fast. After this, dust off the loose charcoal with a chamois skin, or a soft cotton rag, and your picture is ready for the first working with your brushes and paints.

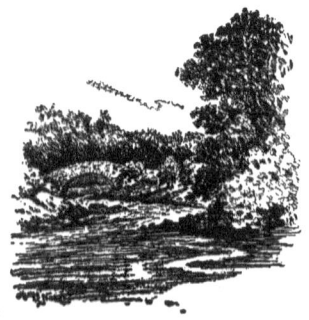

CHAPTER III

MATERIALS RECOMMENDED.

THE materials for an artistic outfit may be elaborate and costly, or simple and inexpensive, according to the tastes or position of the purchaser. The main points are, to get canvases which will not crack or peel off, colours which are durable, work satisfactorily and are pure and true in tint, and brushes which will not disturb your harmony of mind or ruffle your temper as you use them.

Whites. Personally I am using the materials mentioned at the end of this book, and I find them in every way satisfactory. From samples I have seen of the effects of exposure on different makers' Flake Whites, I find that the Flake Whites of Messrs. Reeves & Sons keep the colour best. Therefore, as Flake White is the most important factor in the painting of a picture, whatever the subject may be, I prefer to stick to the white which has stood all the tests known with the best results, and therefore I use, and recommend, the Flake White and other preparations which are manufactured by these makers.

Canvases. With respect to canvases :—There are over twenty samples of different canvases in the pattern book of this firm, and I have tested these patterns in every way I can think of, folding them backwards and forwards (treatment to which no prepared canvases ought to be subjected), yet even under this test the paint has stuck to the fibre without peeling off, and only showing the most minute cracks, after the most brutal roughness and persistence. It stands the strain of the pliers without cracking, to the point of tearing the fabric, and I do not think that even the most particular of ancient masters could expect more endurance ; and, as Messrs. Reeves & Sons are the oldest manufacturers of artists' colours and materials in England, they have had the relentless test of Time to try and prove their excellence, which some of the other makers have yet to be tried by. These therefore are my reasons why I can conscientiously recommend the canvases which I prefer to use myself to those of any other firm.

Personally, I prefer a moderately rough surface such as the single primed ' A ' quality. I like to have as little ground paint on, as possible, for my ground, but this, with the surface, is entirely matter of taste. ' A ' quality is a strong canvas and likely to stand a good deal of straining. ' B ' is a lighter and cheaper quality of canvas, while the cheapest of all are ' J ' and ' N,' which are fairly strong materials and quite suitable for pictures that are not too large.

There are other varieties, such as ' Roman ' and ' Ticken,' with different degrees of grain and roughness, to meet the tastes of dilettantes and art epicures. The important point in getting a canvas is to pick the one that will give you most pleasure in working over it, for that is everything. Some subjects require a rougher surface than others. With landscape and seascape where rugged treatment and force are aimed at, a rough canvas will be of assistance, but for figure subjects and particularly for students who have much correction to do with the charcoal, double primed A and B or single primed B will be found the most suitable. These have just sufficient ' *tooth* ' to take on the charcoal, which can be dusted easily half-out with a feather or hog-hair brush as you go along. Do not paint on a very small canvas, as that may tempt you to use your sables too often, which will get you into a ' niggling ' and weak style ; neither fatigue yourself with too large a size. 14 by 12 inches is a fair size for the smallest, and 36 by 24, is a good limit for the largest. There are a number of sizes and shapes to choose from according to your subject, between those limits.

Easels. The best description of Easel for studio work is undoubtedly one that is upright and can be tilted forward when wanted. Reeves' No. 1 Studio Easel is the cheapest of these, while their No. 6 will answer every requirement of the professional.

For those who do not care to go to the expense of studio easels, a School of Art easel can be obtained for a few shillings. No. 22 of this class is excellent for general work.

For sketching and painting in the open air, there is a large variety of easels in Reeves' price list.

Sketching Stools. The handiest and most easily carried stools are the three and four legged ones, with loose seats; the three legged stools are for gentlemen, and the four legged ones for ladies.

Oil Colour Boxes. The old fashioned tin box is what I use myself, both for in-door and out-door work, and for this I find a size, like No. 323 in the price list, 13 by 8½ inches, quite large enough. You can find your colours easily in this box, which is a great advantage, for nothing is so annoying to

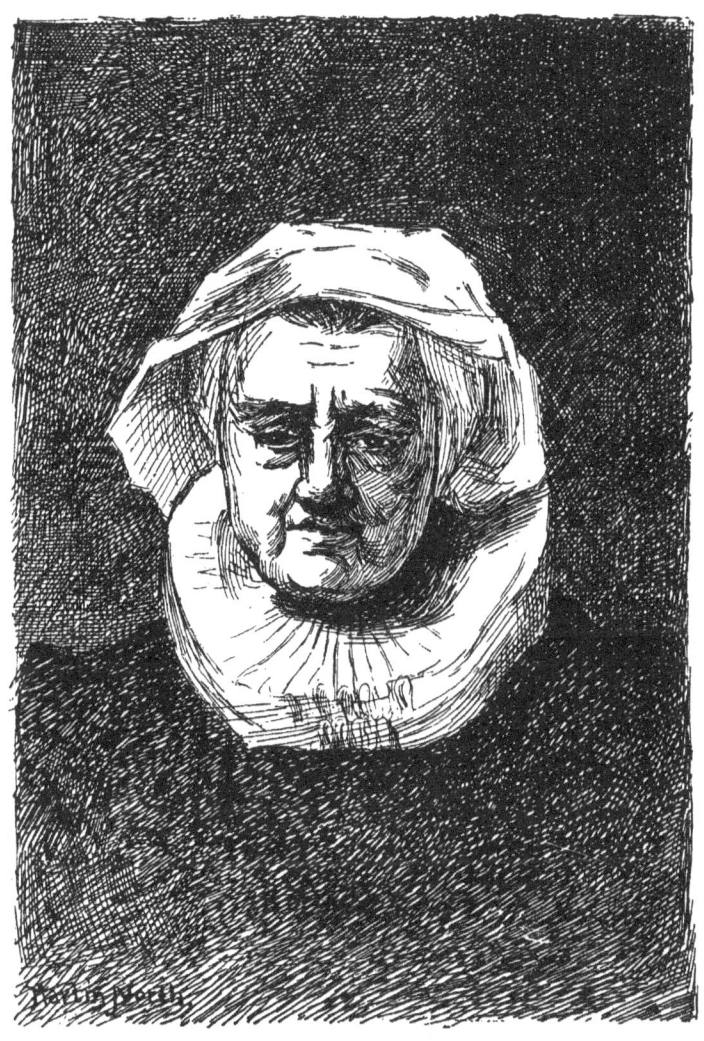

Plate 4

Study after Rembrandt from a
pen drawing by Martin North.

D

the painter as to put off time seeking for the tube he wants, when he is outside trying to catch an effect, and too many colours, in too roomy a box, is a decided waste of time and expenditure of patience and good temper. The tin will dent and get knocked about; therefore to those who like to carry neat baggage I would strongly recommend No. 341, which is about the same size, only made of walnut instead of japanned tin. It is best to purchase the empty box, with palette, dippers, and medium bottles to fit it, and choose your own paints and brushes.

Palettes. You will need one palette, the size of your box, for outside work; for inside work, a couple or three extra palettes, 13 inches or 18 inches, will give you lots of room to mix up your colours.

Brushes. Some painters use a great number of brushes over one working. I like to have a plentiful assortment on my table, *when in the studio*, but as a rule I take a fancy to one, and work with the one I find works smoothly as I want it, all through the day and sometimes nearly all through the picture. I keep a brush-washing dish, filled with turpentine, beside me, with plenty of soft cotton rags to wash and wipe my brush as I need to change the colour-combination. Possibly next day I may discard this brush and take up another, but it is seldom that I have more than half a dozen to wash out when night arrives. I wash my brushes, *myself*, carefully every night, when done with work, using a little extract of soap and hot water, to take out the oil and paint, afterwards rinsing them in several different supplies of clean water and wiping them gently the way of the hair with a clean cotton cloth. My brushes therefore are seldom out of order and never inclined to be ' scrubby.' I wear them a certain way, and wipe them the way they are wearing. A new brush is never so comfortable a companion as one half worn *the proper way*. Also, I'd as soon let another use my tooth brush as the brushes or pen that I work with, either to paint or to wash for me.

You do not require many brushes. Eight hog-hair brushes and five sables are ample to accomplish all sorts of work. Of course as these brushes get worn you will require others to ' break in ' with rough ' rubbing in,' so as to save as much as possible those faithful servitors whom you have used to your hand.

Of these eight hog-hair brushes, provide yourself with four round and four flat brushes. In the round, Nos. 5, 7, 10 and 13. Of the flat, Nos. 4, 7, 10 and 15, with perhaps for extra large work Nos. 18 or 19.

There are some lovely brushes which I use greatly, both for oil and water colour paintings ; these are called the finest Lyons bristles ; yet the Series 101 selected French bristles are good and serviceable. I would not recommend a cheaper quality of brush than this, except for very common purposes.

For ships and tree work, you will find '*riggers*' and '*fans*' at times useful, only you had better work with your flat hog-hairs on foliage than get into the tricky method of using ' fans.'

The sables that you will find useful are Nos. 1 and 4 round, full length hair, Nos. 2, 3 and 4 flat. Use red sables only.

Colours. Messrs. Reeves & Sons have suggested a Palette containing all the principal colours needed, and selected from those that are permanent and may be safely used with each other. I have looked over this Palette carefully and can suggest nothing better, but there are a few other colours which I think should be added to make a thoroughly complete palette. These colours on the palette, placed in their proper order, are as follows : White, Lemon Yellow Pale, Mid. Cadmium, Yellow Ochre, Raw Sienna, Venetian Red, Pale Vermilion, Rose Madder, Alizarin Crimson, Burnt Sienna, Brown Madder, Burnt Umber, Ivory Black, Cobalt Blue, Ultramarine, Viridian.

The colours which I shall add to these are : Aureolin, Antwerp Blue (this is not thoroughly permanent yet it is useful if used with discretion), Caledonian Brown, Terre Verte and Sap Green. I should like also to add Indian Yellow and Brown Pink, but these last two are of doubtful permanency, so that these must be left to your own discretion. Messrs. Reeves & Sons manufacture two qualities of colours, which they style '*Artists*'' colours and ' *Students*'' colours. The '*Artists*'' colours are absolutely pure, the '*Students*'' are more or less adulterated in order to meet the requirements of those who are unable to afford the best article or whose work is of a temporary character only. Do not let some retail tradesman palm off the second quality colours upon you as Reeves' best goods by covering up the original labels with his own.

This separation of the best from the second class ingredients must be a source of greater confidence and security to those artists who pay their money for guaranteed stuff of the best and purest quality ; while as the colours are so closely matched, to beginners, who need not care whether their imperfect efforts endure or not, these second rate pigments supply a great want—the want for stuff cheap enough to come within the limits of students not as yet surfeited with large commissions. Of course *the best is always to be recommended* even for a beginner, if he can afford it. If he cannot however afford the best let him by all means get what he can, so that he may be able to work.

The pigments produced from earths are what a painter mostly has to depend upon throughout his picture. The Ochres :—Yellow and Roman, Venetian and Light Reds, also Terre Verte, Indian Red, Raw and Burnt Siennas, these are all the most useful colours that the palette holds, and are used with the same frequency and lavishness as White throughout the picture.

All colours made from minerals tend towards toning down, and in my estimation it is not a disadvantage in a picture if they darken equally. It is when one colour remains steadfast while the others darken that the original harmony is destroyed, and a little knowledge in chemistry, or, failing that knowledge, a careful study of the analytical table of colours, permanent and fugitive, at the beginning of Reeves' price list, will prevent you from making any mistake. There is here a very extensive range of colours, of all the shades required to paint any picture, which you can use with safety. My advice therefore is, keep to the safe colours and accustom yourself to the use of them only, from the beginning ; and so, never knowing the use of the fugitive tints, you will not miss them, and your picture, although not perhaps quite so luscious and glowing, as it may be with the use of the transparent, but treacherous, vegetable glazes, when first finished, will in the course of time reward you and the purchaser of it, by remaining as you finished it, with the added glazings which age alone can impart to it, instead of becoming a faded and unequal blotch. Gainsborough was wise in his generation, and preferred to leave his glazings in the hands of the finisher Time; whereas his contemporary Reynolds, and, later, Turner, seduced by their passion for luscious colouring, made each picture a *tour de force* which dazzled the eyes of their immediate contemporaries, and left to the succeeding generations only pallid spectres of what were, in their first flush of youth, startling beauties. *Ergo*, be wise even in your student attempts; keep to the earths and the minerals which will mix together without angering each other, and all will grow mellow with age in company; and avoid, as much as you can, those prismatic and evanescent sirens, the vegetable extracts and the cochineals. In which case it will not matter so much whether you have to use the Art Students' preparations, until you can afford to indulge in the carefully selected Artists' colours.

There are Lakes, delicious enough to tempt even the wisest and most prudent of Artists to frolic with—Italian Lake and Yellow Lake. Turner doted on such-like indulgences, even although he must have known that they would murder his conceptions. There are Browns, so rich and transparent that one has to lay them aside with a groan of discontent, for no other browns can do what they can do. Of this class are the preparations of Asphaltum ; so deep and lustrous they are, that with but little trouble we can produce almost the marvellous mysteries of that unapproachable master of colour, Rembrandt ; but alas ! if we are bewitched into making use of this siren of the Dead Sea, our triumph will be a short lived one, for our picture may be irretrievably ruined ; therefore we must be content with the more opaque and homely Caledonian and Van-dyke Browns. Brown Madder, however, with Raw Sienna, does not make a bad substitute for Asphaltum when adroitly used.

Sundry articles required. The palette knife is an indispensable article which no painter can be without. Also a mahl stick to rest the hand when putting in details. These, with plenty of old soft cotton rags, Turpentine, Medium, Megilp, or a little Copal Varnish, and if you wish to make your paints dry very quickly, Japan Gold size, or Drying

Oil (only be careful in your use of driers, as they all tend to damage and disintegrate, as well as crack your colours), with a little Poppy or Nut Oil to moisten your picture between the different workings—these, with a box of charcoal, will complete your outfit as a painter in oils.

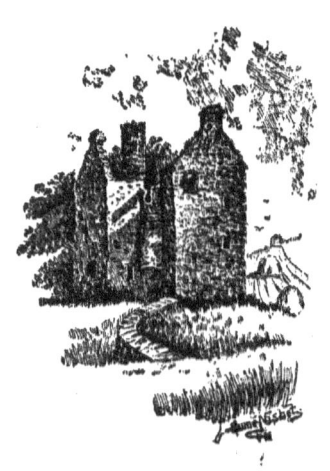

CHAPTER IV.

FIRST WORKING OF FIGURE SUBJECTS.

I HAVE looked over the different palettes used by modern painters of repute, with the directions left by those old masters who have given records of their secrets, and here give you a comprehensive palette which will meet all the strict requirements of the art of figure painting. They are as follows :

Flake White, Yellow Ochre, Raw Sienna, Pale Vermilion, Venetian Red, Rose Madder, Raw Umber, Burnt Sienna, Brown Madder, Caledonian or Vandyke Brown, Cobalt, Ivory Black, and Terre Verte.

These colours are placed, in the order written, on the outer edge of the palette, from the thumb-hole half-way round the palette, thus giving you plenty of space to mix your tints.

You have drawn your subject, boldly and firmly, yet carefully, in with your pencil over the charcoal, and dusted the charcoal marks as much out as you can. The first thing to do after this is to *dirty* your canvas so as to bring down its tone, otherwise its glaring will possibly make you start with too high a scale of colour which will give you no end of trouble to reduce afterwards. Remember that it is always much easier to elevate the tone of your picture than it is to reduce it; therefore keep it dark and subdued in tone as long as you can, and reserve your highest lights to the finishing touches. Another safe rule is to strive never to put white on purely even on the highest light of a white collar, shirt or dress; rather make it appear white by contrast with the other colours near it.

To dirty your canvas, take a little Venetian Red and Raw Umber on a hog-hair brush : using Nos. 3 and 8 for this process, with as much medium as will make these colours more or less transparent, so that you can see your lines through them. Use your colours as dry as you can to produce the transparency necessary. A good and safe medium is made by mixing copal varnish and linseed oil in equal parts, with just sufficient turpentine to make them thin enough. If however the weather is cold, and damp, and you want your canvas to be dry enough to begin working next day, put less oil into the varnish.

Some books on painting advise Mastic Varnish, but this is altogether wrong; the only use mastic varnish is for in pictures is to varnish them after they are completely finished, if the colours have

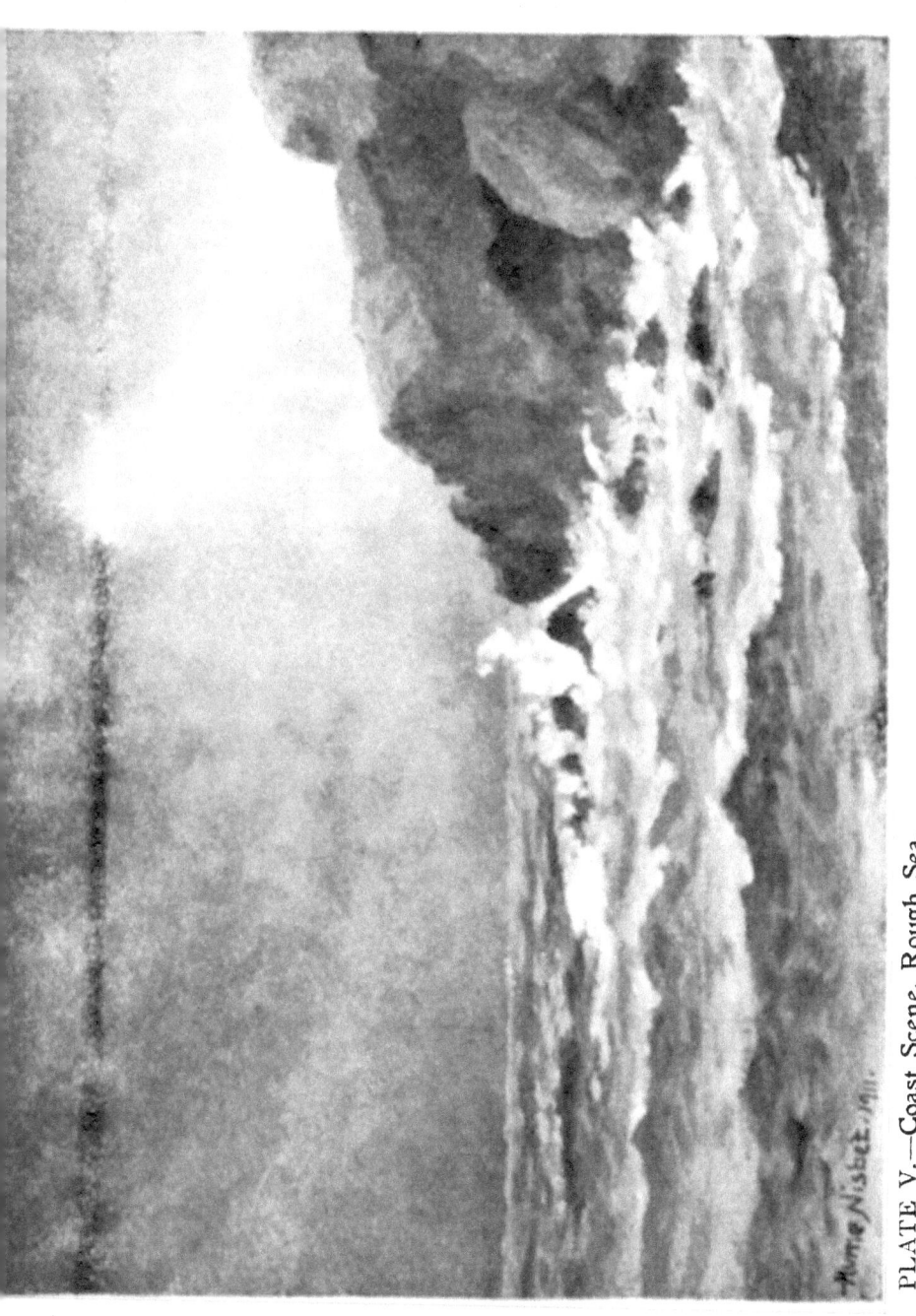

PLATE V.—Coast Scene, Rough Sea.

become dim ; even then, a little medium or poppy oil rubbed over and dried off with a silk handkerchief is better. A picture ought never to be varnished until it has stood at least for a twelve-month drying and '*sweating*,' *i.e.*, until the oils have all come, or sweated, to the surface. Then a coat of thin mastic varnish will preserve the paints and protect them from the dirt and atmospheric deterioration.

Mastic varnish being made from turpentine and a gum, can be lifted from the picture, when it is cleaned, with spirits of wine. If you use it in your painting or glazing, then these also will be in danger of coming away with the outer coating of varnish, and, as in many pictures by Reynolds and other portrait painters, your delicate work will be destroyed ; besides this, it is apt to ' clog ' in the drying, and dry too quickly and unequally while you are working on it, which is bad.

Now copal varnish is made by dissolving the gum in oil,* so that after it is thoroughly dry spirits of wine will not touch it easily, and the picture may be cleaned with impunity, losing nothing in the process. It also dries slowly and regularly, not in eddies as mastic varnish does, when it is worked upon while 'tacky,' *i.e.*, sticky.

* There is also a varnish known as Copal Spirit Varnish to which I do not refer.

Copal Varnish also unites more kindly with the colours. For these reasons I advise its use, and repudiate what some of the other text books, which I have glanced over, so unpractically advise.

Use no white in this 'scumbling' or dirtying process, but rub your paint hard out over the high lights and half-tones, wiping half out, with a piece of rag, the highest lights if you have made them too dark ; this however you can do after you have ' dirtied ' it all over.

Your picture will be a warm tinted monochrome when done. Try to get your effects of light and shadow in this warm sepia-like tone, as those will help you greatly in your first colour working ; but, while you put in the shadows and half-tones boldly, do not make them opaque, but let the canvas shine through even your deepest shadows. Work your edges between the lights, half-lights, and shadows, softly and vaguely, and merge your figures gently into the background, so that when you stand back from your canvas, the picture will steal out dreamily and softly, with nothing harsh about it. To do this successfully, as I have already said, only dip your brushes into your medium when they get too dry to work comfortably, and ' scrub ' over your canvas as firmly as you can, wiping your brush on your rag first, when you want to take some of the half shadows out, and lastly wiping with the clean rag, round the point of your forefinger or thumb, those parts where the very highest lights fall, leaving a slight stain even on these highest lights. The thumb of an artist is one of the most sensitive tools he can use.

If you carry out this stage properly, your picture ought to have the broad effect of chiaroscuro which you intend it to have when finished. You have also now the full opportunity of being able to know definitely whether your previous measurements have been correct, and if you have left room enough for your shadows and roundings. Shadows and protuberances are so apt to deceive one when drawing objects in relief and outline on a flat surface. Your outlines, before the shadows are filled in, always appear too big. That is why I have impressed upon you the strict necessity of making your outer lines as large and broad as your measurements will permit you, in order to make room for the shadows.

Before leaving your canvas for the day or night to dry, place it alongside of your models or sitter and get as far back from them both as you can, then study them carefully and critically. If any alteration has to be made, make it if possible now, as it is so much easier to correct faults in the drawing than it will be when you begin to colour.

If it meets your approval, leave well alone and place it with its face against the wall to dry against the morrow.

Do not pay any heed to people who may tell you that all this work is unnecessary. You will find that it has not been lost labour, before you are finished, from the ease and confidence it will give you in your future workings. In the drawing of the outline and staining in of the shadows you cannot be too careful and patient if you desire to produce a painting worth being looked at.

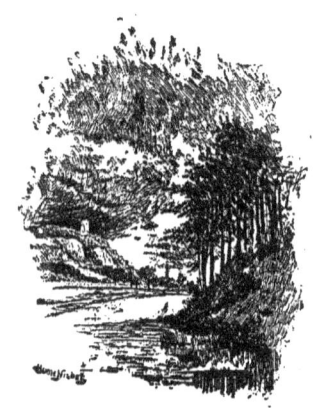

CHAPTER V.

THE PRACTICE OF STILL LIFE AND THE COPYING OF GOOD PICTURES FOR STYLE.

OF course my readers will understand that, before tackling living subjects, it will be strictly needful for them to accustom themselves to the ' Round ' by making studies from still life.

A collection of china, or articles of virtu, with some drapery artistically arranged will be the best for this purpose, besides making interesting pictures when done. Painting in monochrome also, from antique busts and figures, will be found of infinite use, as these masterpieces of grace and proportion will teach you what human perfection is ; yet on the whole the student who draws from the Greek statues has a much more difficult task than the student who draws from the life.

Copying, as well as looking often at pictures by great masters, will be found of immense educative value, as he will learn some of the technique as

F.

well as manner in which those masters approached and treated nature. In our National Galleries there are many pictures which I could point out as the most useful for the young painter to study with his eye, if he cannot get a copying ticket, or may not have leisure on the days appointed for copying.

I am not a great admirer of the early masters, with their bad drawing and their ugly ideals of Madonnas and such like monstrosities. The much extolled Botticelli fails to interest me, although I do rather like his definite outlines. The pictures in the Gallery by Raffaelle, with the exception of the portrait of the Pope, I consider of no earthly value to a student who wants to be a painter.

Velasquez however is good and strong, and a young artist will not be wasting his time by copying one of his portraits. Likewise Murillo. Moroni, whose ' Tailor' is here reproduced (*see* Figure 3)—in my opinion the most realistic and restrained piece of work in the National Gallery—must improve the student. Rembrandt, the magnificent, will reveal to him wonders in the way of colour and depth of shadow, although his touch is impossible to get hold of. The ' Head of an Old Woman ' (Figure 4), which also forms one of our illustrations, is the easiest study to copy of the several portraits by this great master, also one where the handling can best be comprehended. The others are impossible to reproduce in line drawing, by reason of their profound depth and mystery.

If you will study these pictures carefully, and then turn from the works of these dead Masters to the works of one of our living Masters that can bear comparison with any of them, I mean those great portraits by Watts which adorn the walls of the National Portrait Gallery, you will be all the more capable of approaching and appreciating the subtilty of life.

I do not approve of too much copying of other men's work, no matter how great they are, as such practice, if too long continued, will enslave a student. A little however is of use. Make a careful selection of those works that interest you the most, as the styles which attract you are the promptings of a style that is at present latent in you. If the strong and rugged work appeals to you, don't try to admire the smoothly finished or soft, simply because you may be advised to admire it. It may be good and right for someone else It does not suit you. Permit your inclination to be your guide in your choice of subjects and manner, and follow it out conscientiously and faithfully, and you will make rapid progress. Be in love earnestly with your subject, and you must paint it better than if you look upon it only as a duty.

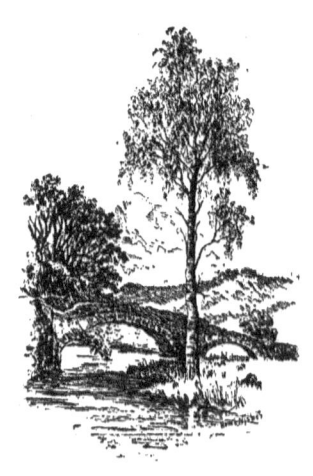

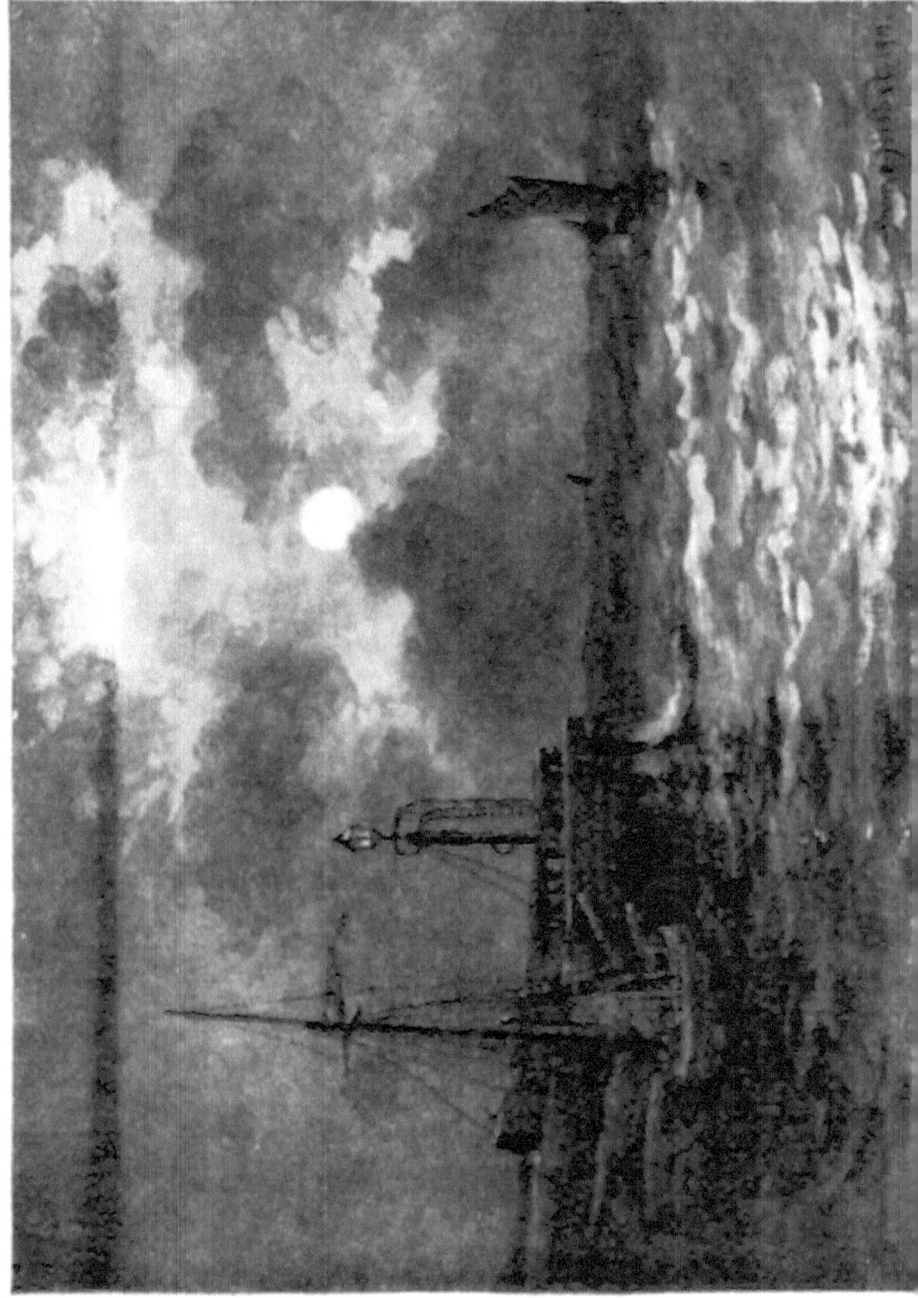

CHAPTER VI.

THE FIRST WORKING IN COLOUR OF FIGURE SUBJECTS.

YOU have decided upon your chiaroscuro and positions and are satisfied with your drawing and shading. The next point to consider before setting your palette is how you wish to treat it—if in a fine, pains-taking, and smoothly finished style, or in the heavily built-up and rugged style. Both systems are to be admired when properly done, and, as the fine and thinly painted manner is likely to be most popular, I will touch upon that first.

Orchardson is perhaps one of the best examples to hold up for you to follow ; also Alma Tadema with his high finish and elaborate detail.

Look at your subject as if it were a patchwork of different colours, or a bit of mosaic, instead of a human face. Try first to separate the colours, and when you have done so, for instance on the brow, pick out one nearest to the highest light and measure mentally its size and shape, then dip your brush into the white, place that daub in the centre of your palette and mix it with Yellow Ochre and Venetian Red, with perhaps a little Umber or Terre Verte, until it gets what you reckon to be a couple of shades darker, yet of the same tone as the colours of your original, and put that upon the exact portion of your copy, in as nearly the same shape and size in proportion, as it appears to be on the subject. This patch will be your keynote for the rest of the face.

Do not be discouraged or frightened if it looks a dirty patch where you have placed it. Possibly before you have finished your first working it will be too startlingly light.

The first working ought to be a series of detached mosaic or patches of distinct and varied tints, broadly and definitely placed side by side with each other, and so closely that there is no division between them, yet never mixing. Good colour means keeping your paints pure and separate, and mixing them up as little as possible.

It is impossible to lay down fixed rules as to what colours to use on the different parts of a face or body.

When you have learnt the art of making secondary and tertiary tints—that is, how to blend oranges, purples and greens, and to make the different varieties of grey—you must experiment until you get just the tints you want.

White, Yellow and Red will make a flesh tint, Yellow Ochre and Venetian Red it may be on some parts, Ochre and Vermilion on others or Ochre and Rose Madder on other portions, such as the lips, cheeks and flushed places. You can also use Cadmium and Rose Madder with White for any bright portions of the complexion.

Terre Verte, Raw Sienna and Rose Madder produce a silvery grey ; or if you like use Naples Yellow instead of the Sienna ; but you can make grey with a number of the other primaries and secondaries : Cobalt Blue, Rose Madder, and Ochre ; Cobalt, Vermilion and Ochre ; Cobalt and Venetian Red with Ochre, Sienna or Umber ; Cobalt, Raw Sienna and Brown Madder ; Ivory Black and White. The greys are infinite, and are in no picture absent from everything that has colour.

You have placed your highest light on the forehead. Paint round and from that with varying degrees of flesh colour, impregnated with grey of which you will see different kinds on every face if you look carefully—violet-grey, not too pronounced of course in the original, but you must accentuate it more in your painting at this stage. To make this violet-grey, use Cobalt and Rose Madder, or Vermilion, Light Red or Brown Madder with the Cobalt and a little of your last flesh tint, for this violet-grey half-tone must be a shade under your last flesh touch.

Some faces gather about them blue or colder shadows than others. When you have such a face to copy, try to imitate the tones which you see on the shadow part of an oyster shell or a pearl. Venetian Red and Cobalt, with the faintest touch of Raw Sienna, will make a very delicious pearly shade.

Some faces have, besides more violent purples, a good deal of divided green and saffron stains about them. These will be more easy to copy than the delicate ones, because all the colours are so positive that you do not need to search for them. You can make what looks like a dirty grey appear either greenish or pearly with the colours you place next to it, so that there is no need for you to go muddling and mixing the colour you have just put on in order to make it purer. Remember that much mixing and dabbling will always make colours both dirty and waxy. If therefore your grey appears too umbery, you can make it appear purple by putting more yellow, *i.e.*, Raw Sienna or Ochre, into the tint next to it ; or you can make it greenish by using Brown Madder in your next tint. In this way you bring down your lights to the shadows by soft gradations of colours placed in direct juxtaposition with each other, yet never worked into each. They must be kept separate if you desire to be true and pure in your style.

As this is a smooth painting I am describing, do not load your canvas with paint, yet always put enough on to cover the canvas in the lights so that it does not show through, and also leave no hard edges. Place your colours daintily and deliberately upon the canvas with *one* stroke if possible—a soft brush stroke, with the paint thick enough to lie smoothly on, leaving only sufficient *texture*, *i.e.*, brush marks, to *grip* your next working.

You will not attempt to get a likeness in this working, or go into any small details such as hairs, eye-brows or eye-lashes ; all that you must aim at is to get the colours, *in masses*, of these parts, with their shadows.

I expect, however, if you keep faithfully to your drawing and reproduce the colours in their reduced scale with fidelity, that although you are not thinking about the likeness, unconsciously you will produce a very good if vague likeness even in this working, and when you stand back from it far enough to lose sight of the want of details, you will be astonished at your own success.

While you are working, place your picture every now and again alongside of your sitter, and you will be able to judge your progress with greater certainty. If you have a looking glass handy, look at the picture in that also at times. It will reverse the picture and give you a fresh appearance of it which may reveal some shortcoming or oversight which you have not observed before.

As you approach the deeper shadows, use your colours more thinly and transparently, leaving the deepest shadows with only a thin *scumble* or glaze over them. This will give you a greater depth and more transparency about the deep shadows, which in most faces will be found to be rich and warm in tone, *i.e.*, reddish and brown. Brown Madder and Raw Sienna mixed will give you the transparency you require, while the slight scumble of this body colour will appear cool and grey over your previous shading.

The hair and beard you will put on as you have done the flesh : the light parts and half lights, with solid colour darker than the original ; the minor shadows thinly and semi-transparent ; the deepest shadows altogether transparent or glazed in.

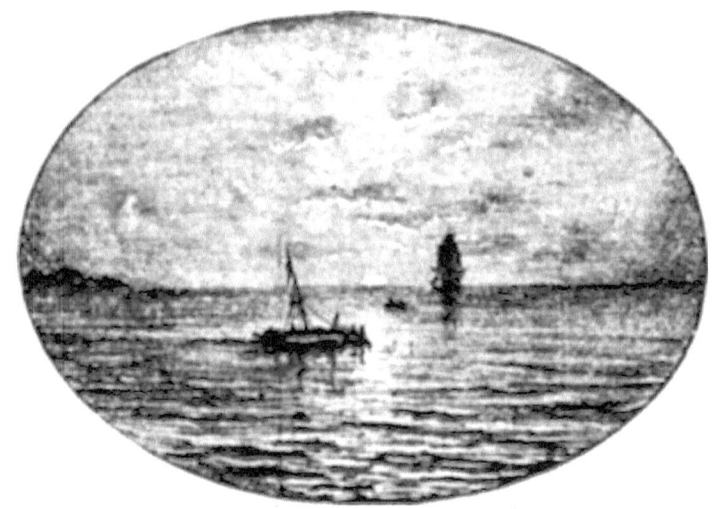

DRAPERY.

WHITE drapery you must keep very much down in tone; this advice applies to all light-coloured drapery. Look out for your shadows and folds, and play as much of the primary colours about them as possible. Raw Sienna, Umber, Terre Verte, Rose Madder and Cobalt, for all these colours couch very purely amongst the folds and shadows of white; a little grey scumbled over your light parts will be white enough just now. It is a great triumph won if you can restrain and keep yourself well under control at this stage, and in fact through all the stages. You are the Master, while you do so, of your paints and of your effect as well. Your light colours should be your aces, and, like trump-cards, kept back till the end, when you can play them, if they need to be played; but probably you will win the game without requiring to use them at all.

This is the golden rule of Painting in Oils. Have always in reserve at the least a couple of degrees of light; also do what you can with your shadows as regards depth one or two degrees above blackness. Bear in mind the inexorable fact that you cannot possibly get higher than Flake White, nor lower than Black—these two extremes must finish and stop you ; yet, by keeping well within the limits, you may create illusions of light by adroit and subtle contrasts, which will appear much more luminous than White, and, by transparent glazings, appearances of deeper darkness than pure Black could give you. In these contrasts and harmonies lie all the secrets of the great colourist.

All Yellow and Orange draperies cast purple shadows of various degrees.

All Red draperies throw green shadows.

All Green draperies cast reddish or warm shadows.

Blue draperies cast brown shadows.

Brown draperies cast blue shadows.

Purple draperies gather yellow tones in their folds and shadows.

Grey draperies will cast warm shadows ; if purple grey, the shadows will be tawny ; if greenish grey, they will be more russet, and so forth. Whatever is the colour you are using, as the local colour of the object you are painting, take as your shadow a modification of the colours which are absent in its own composition.

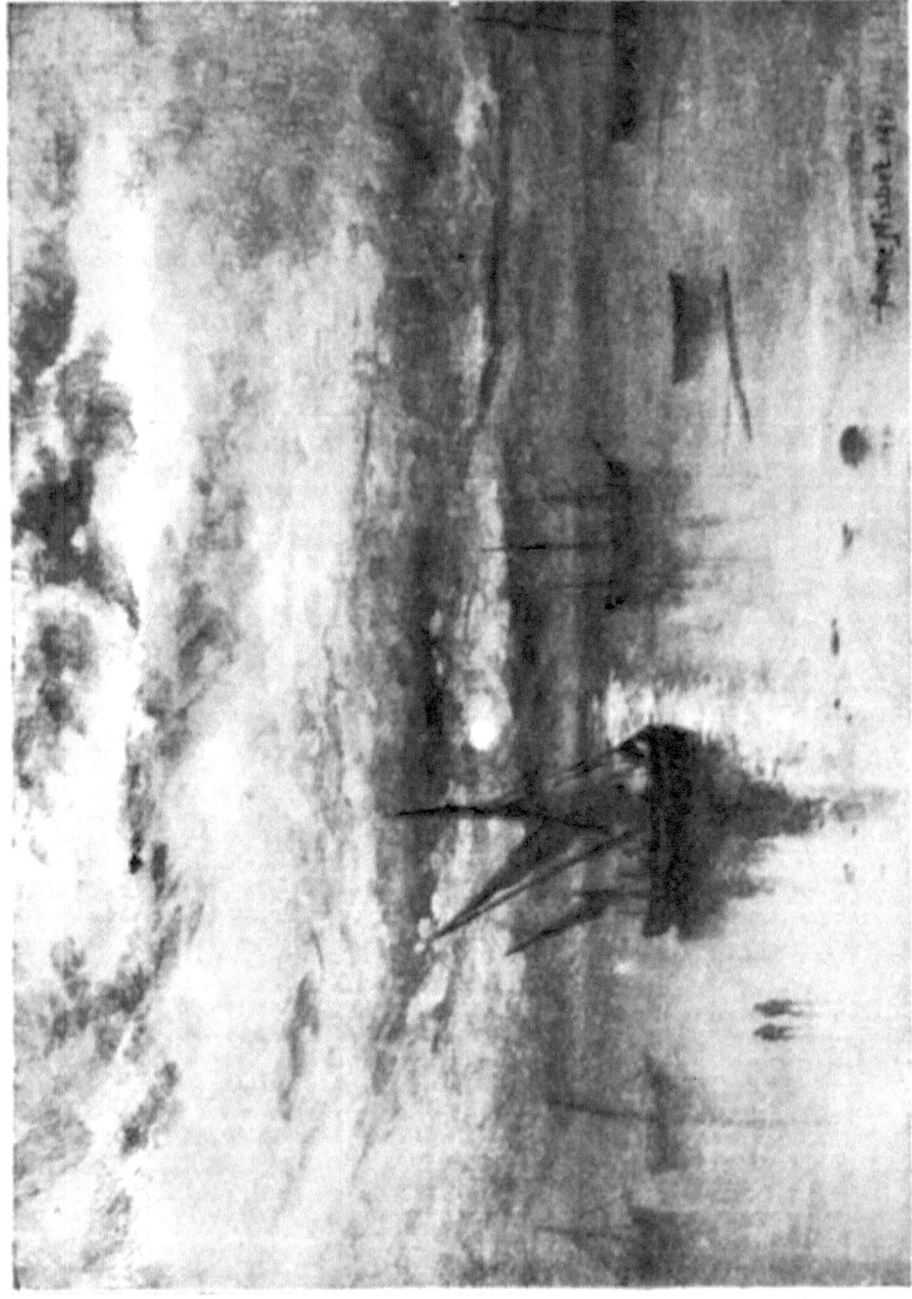

Red, blue and yellow* are your primaries ; if one of these predominate in your masses, the other two must be found playing amongst the shadows or in their proximity.

Not violently of course, for Nature does not assert her contrasts crudely, but in a subtle and hidden way which has to be searched for keenly, and found out by the painter.

In the painting of folds, at this stage, put in only the largest and most important, leaving the smaller folds and creases to be painted in the after working with the other details. The deepest shadows, leave as transparent as you can.

Lace, and such-like articles of costume, do not attempt even to suggest at this stage, but paint the dress over which they lie, as if for the time they had been taken off.

* I allude to Red, Blue and Yellow as primaries solely from the painter's point of view, and not from the stand-point of strict science.

ACCESSORIES AND BACKGROUNDS.

THE considerations which should first occupy the attention of a painter are his composition, the story or fact he wishes to tell, and the objects that have to tell it.

Thus, if he has a figure, this figure must occupy the stage and keep the interest of the spectators ; and all other objects and accessories in the picture must play subordinate parts, as they are placed there only to help this principal character, not to distract attention from him. If a set of figures are together in the picture, one must play the leading part while the others have to play for his or her benefit. Even where only a couple are represented, they cannot both speak at once, and in a picture only one has the opportunity to engage the attention of the audience from first to last.

Composition. This is where composition and selection come in, and the painter must make up his mind what has to be his principal character, as he has also to decide upon his principal light and shadow, make all the other portions more or less subordinate to this choice, and never deviate afterward from his first decision. This is a law which can no more be violated than can the laws of perspective.

His first care will be devoted to this central object. He may render it conspicuous by a greater amount of finish or detail, if he does not wish it to engross the strongest light. Or it may be by something peculiar or striking about the costume or expression, but whatever ruse he adopts, that figure will arrest the attention of the spectator, either forcibly or gently, yet always irresistibly, otherwise the painter has transgressed the first principles of composition, and is likely to suffer for his sins by missing his point and failing to interest anyone.

Now, where many pictures are spoilt is not through carelessness so much as from over attention being bestowed upon the subordinates and accessories. The painter has a fine and elaborate cabinet or curio in his picture, and he falls so deeply in love with it, and he dwells upon it with such tender and detailed care, that the curio asserts its right to be looked at, with equal if not more pertinacity, than the actor who is supposed to be claiming attention. Beware of being too greatly in love with more than one object in each picture; rather paint that curio by itself, if you must elaborate it.

Lately I went through the Campo Santo in Genoa, where I saw some of the most deplorable specimens of sculpture work on the monuments—

drapery and lace so assertively carved that it was almost impossible to see any other point about the statues—and I was able only to carry away with me the memory of one simply draped figure broadly sculptured, amid a wild confusion of prettily carved lace trimmings.

In your painting of accessories, keep them well under, and paint them broadly and without ostentation. If you watch them keenly, Nature will teach you how to paint them, for, no matter what their original colour, texture or elaboration may be, they must lose their detail when contrasted with the principal figure, and become clothed, by juxtaposition, with the colours that are necessary to contrast and bring out this principal object. That is, either they must do so, or it will have to yield to them, for two objects cannot dispute the supremacy or even equality in one picture, any more than they can agree together on equal ground in life. If you keep this in your mind you will save yourself much useless labour and vexation, as well as wonderment what it is that has gone wrong with your picture, after it is finished. The painting of these accessories and subordinates ought to be, in various degrees, as broad, simple and full of shadow transparency as possible.

Backgrounds. This is a portion of the picture that, by the commonplace artist and the beginner, is too often erroneously regarded as of very minor importance; and yet it is exactly here where the great colourist revels and expends all his knowledge and restrained powers; for by painting the background with skill the artist alone can give the true values of harmony, contrast, and force to his figures. It is here where all your knowledge of colour and subtle gradations are required, where you can play your scales of colour and variety of tones amongst the shadows, and echo, as well as accentuate and harmonize, all the different colours of flesh, hair and costume, in your figures and the surrounding accessories.

Your background is not merely a blank space to be filled up with any colour or shadow tint which may be handy on your palette, as so many seem to consider it, but a void which may be filled with harmonies, delicate suggestions, repetitions, and accompaniments to the composition which you have created; or it is a void which will become blanker and more meaningless with the dirt you daub over it.

To paint it as it ought to be painted, you will require every colour, in a more subdued and disguised key, which you have on your lights and in your shadows, throughout every object of your picture, with their different complementray and contrasting tones beside. Every brush mark must

F

be altered with the same deliberation with which you laid on the dead colour of the flesh and costumes, &c., to suit whatever is in juxtaposition with it. This may chance to be a whitewashed wall, or the time-stained panels and dusky shadows of a wainscoted chamber. It may be a modern wall-paper or an ancient hanging of tapestry; the task before you is to paint, by broad suggestion which will not intrude, the local colour and pattern or design, and also blend them harmoniously with the echoes and contrasts of your picture.

I cannot tell you how to do this further than by saying, paint the background exactly as you have painted the other portions of your picture, only much more deliberately, thoughtfully and cunningly, studying every object all round with every touch so that you may best give the interest value to what you have already painted in; and if you do not quite succeed, for only the very greatest and most experienced of colourists can do this up to a limit, you will at least have produced something that will reward your labour, and will have discovered secrets of colour that must advance your next work.

The backgrounds of Sir John Millais appear rough and unfinished to the uneducated eye, but they possess this quality. Rembrandt's backgrounds have often more labour and care bestowed upon them than his figures have Orchardson's backgrounds may be quoted as samples of what I have now tried to describe.

The Value of Space. There is nothing more difficult to a painter than the leaving of spaces or room in his picture. The constant temptation is to crowd a composition. If you go into any exhibition you may see a picture here and there with space enough about it to give elbow room to the figures, and a sense of repose to the spectator, yet the majority of the exhibits are crammed full of objects.

It takes a great deal of experience, as well as a masterly firmness of purpose, before a painter can learn the full value of isolation and space, and yet there is nothing which proves the strength and greatness of a painter more than this, to know the exact limit which the subject and the spectator can stand in the way of room and be bold enough to give it. I again quote Orchardson as the best living exponent of space, as he is one of the most refined of colourists. If you look at his pictures carefully, the first impression will possibly be, that you would like to have something to break up those large spaces which he leaves; the second and lasting impression is, that you don't want anything to disturb the reposeful feeling which is settling upon you and bringing you right into the picture. With most other pictures you are forced to stand outside and look at the actors from a distance, but with Orchardson's pictures you seem to take your stand, or sit down, with the characters and to study them at your leisure. You look round critically, and say to yourself with a sigh of infinite satisfaction, 'This is nice and restful, but another sixteenth of an inch left and it would have been dreary and comfortless.' That is where this Master shows his courage and his skill : he knows exactly how far he dare go in the way of isolation, but he goes his utter length and just stops in time.

In those spaces however, so colourless seemingly, and bleached out to faint grey, he exhibits his full force as a subtle colourist : they *vibrate* with delicious and delicate variations, and as your eye watches these frequent spaces so redolent of sensitive colours and silvery purity, if gifted at all with the instinct of poetic colour, you seem to be sitting within a vast chamber, flooded in subdued light, and listening to the distant tremblings of Æolian harps. This is exactly the effect which i wish you to feel and attempt to reproduce in your backgrounds. In your compositinns, aim always to have as much room as you can get, without producing the effect of emptiness or barrenness.

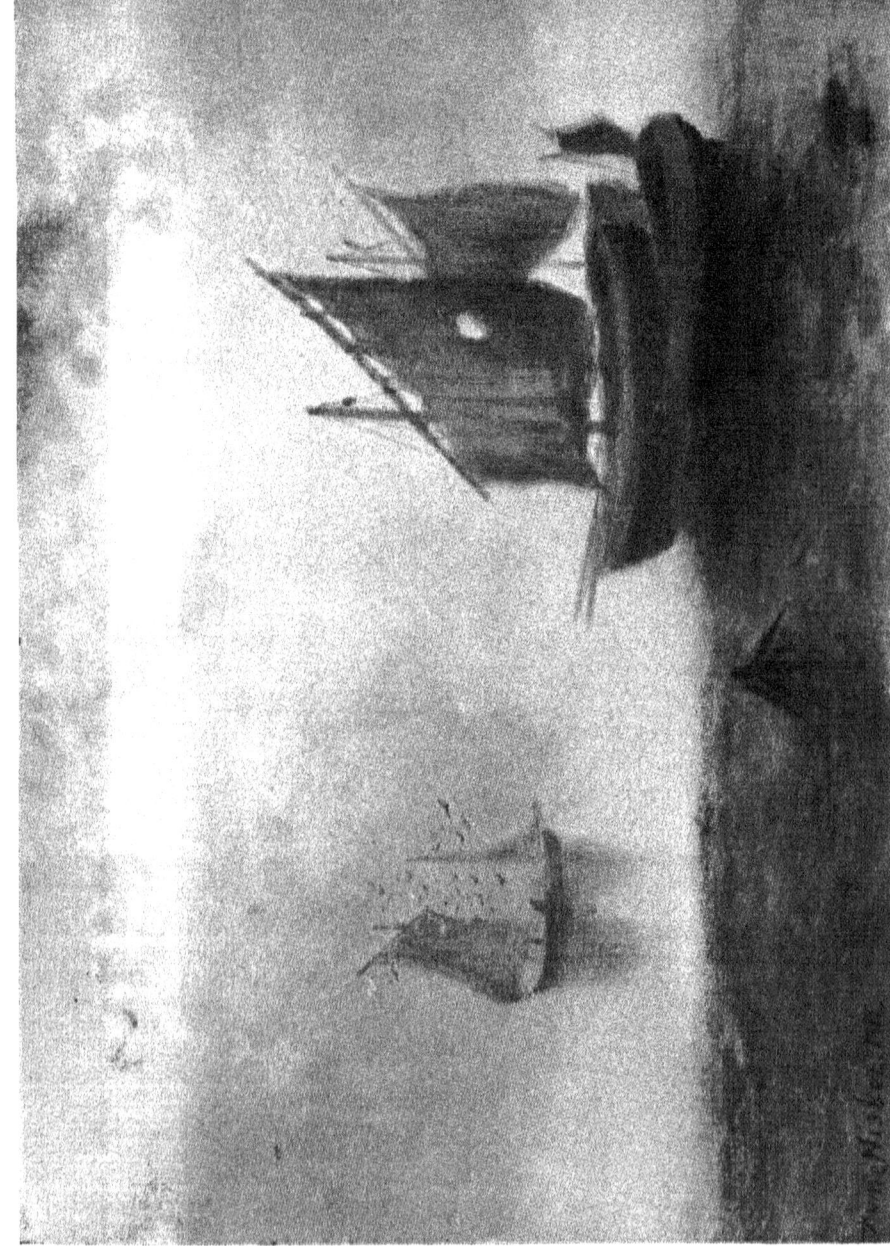

THE MASSIVE STYLE OF PAINTING.

As smooth and light painting suits some minds the bold and massive style of painting commends itself to others. Painters who take to this kind of work are of more robust and less refined minds. They will most likely be stern realists and Zolas of art. The poetic and romantic will not so much appeal to them, as the strong and rugged. Their subjects will be drawn from everyday life, and their work will be materialistic, vivid and open aired.

Luke Fildes in his 'Widower' is a fair specimen of this class, who like to build up their pictures with solid and heavy layers of paint and depend upon a good deal of their effects by texture.

To paint in this way you will begin the first working exactly as you would do with the other style, only instead of placing your colours softly you will place them side by side heavily, using your colours as dry as you can, *i.e.*, just as you squeeze them from your tubes without thinning them with medium, or if you want to thin them at all, use turpentine only, in very spare doses. The prominences and corrugations, place on your canvas as if you want to make a low relief of your picture.

It requires considerable practice to do this properly, for the roughnesses and coarse brush marks must not be laid on at random, but made to follow the roughnesses of Nature exactly, with the textures of the different articles. All sorts of tricks must be resorted to as you go along : your palette knife used sometimes as a plasterer would lay on plaster with a trowel, your fingers at other times, or you may carve out a wrinkle with a sharp pointed stick, smoothing some portions while you leave others standing out boldly, yet artfully, from the canvas.

All the while you must be most particular to get your tints correctly ; indeed this first working has to be carried on much farther than the first working of a smooth painting, for you are carving, as well as painting.

There must be no transparent shadows left, *i.e.*, no portion where the canvas can show through. This transparency and depth you will get by subsequent glazings. Your task at present is to cover the canvas solidly and heavily from end to end.

You may strike a higher key in your lights and in places put on the white purely if you like. It will be found better to lay on your strongest lights in dead white, and work your other colours lightly amongst the white on your picture without mixing the tints on your palette at all.

For example, place a thick daub of white, straight from the tube, on to the lightest part of the forehead, then take a touch of ochre and dash it over the white ; after that take Rose Madder and qualify the ochre, tone down this combination with Terre Verte or Cobalt and go on with your blendings, and shading off with thick daubs of pure colour on the canvas direct. The effect you will find to be very dazzling and prismatic, yet, when seen at the right distance, very realistic and true to the brilliance of your model.

As you paint your lights in a high key, you must put in your shadows in the same way, much lighter and clearer than you intend them to be when finished. Make your contrasts violent, strong and brilliant, the purples, greens, yellows and reds more intense and crude. The carmine on the cheeks and lips should be juicy and glowing, the shadow blendings of Raw Sienna and Brown Madder qualified in the grey parts with Terre Verte and Cobalt all blended, *but not too much mixed together*, amongst the white ; they should rather run through it, in vivid and separate veins and streaks, which cross over each other to produce the colour wanted as the thread of a tartan does.

Work on this first working as long as you can improve it, but do not muddle the colours together, or the result will be disastrous; also carry it as far as you can before you set it away to dry. The first working is complete when you have produced a glowing and consistent harmony all through, with the texture of the flesh and other articles as they are in the original, all suggested, as far as they can be suggested, without the finer details.

When you are satisfied that you can do no more at this stage, put it away and begin on another subject, for your picture must be thoroughly dry before you can touch it again, and it may take weeks to dry hard enough.

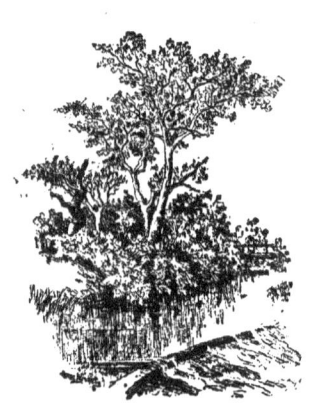

CHAPTER VII.

FIRST WORKING OF LANDSCAPES.

WHEN you first attempt to paint Landscape in the open air, you will find even the simplest corner so complex, so filled with varieties of form and colour, that you may be tempted to give it up as a hopeless task. You get into such a muddle or confusion that there seems to be no way out of it.

On the whole, perhaps a large and extensive landscape will be found easier to imitate, *after a style,* by a beginner, than even a selected corner, because in your very blundering over the ground you may give it a breadth and simplicity, by accident, which you may try vainly to reproduce when you are farther advanced.

Once a pupil of advanced years came to me to get lessons in water colour. Why he came I can hardly tell, because he was so short-sighted that he was forced to use the most powerful glasses before he could see to read even the largest book type ; as for seeing Nature farther away than a few inches that was impossible to him. I explained, as well as I could, how to blend his colours, and then, taking him to the open window of my studio,

I told him to try to copy what he saw, and then I would be able to judge whether he had any gift at all for painting. I asked him if he could see any form, and he answered that he could not ; what he did see seemed to be a blur of soft colours. I told him to paint that blur if he could, then I sat down to watch him working. He placed his colour box very close to his eyes and then he began, only asking me a question now and then as to what colours he should take to produce a certain tint, or how moist he should make his paper. He worked slowly, but kept his paper wet as I instructed him.

I was astonished at his adaptability and the ease with which he managed after a little time to blend his colours. I must believe also that he reproduced what he saw correctly and purely, thereby proving him to be a born colourist, for the result was the most delicious play of colour blendings that I ever saw. The scene before him was a crowded street, and he gave me a vague *impression* of that crowd and street as if a soft semi-transparent mist had fallen over it. I could not have wished a more perfect specimen of first working, either in oils or water colours, than this gentleman gave me in his first sketch.

However, as I do not wish you to do any work by chance, particularly when you are beginning, you will do best to fix upon a subject as simple and plain in its character as you can find, yet with sufficient of the picturesque about it to make it interesting to you. An old wall might be good practice, for like a background, it has a wealth of colour about it ; yet as it will not make a very interesting picture by itself when done, perhaps you had better decide upon a subject when you can have all that the old wall will give you and a little form as well.

I have drawn out a progressive set of studies as guides for you in the descriptions of subjects you ought to look out for before attempting anything widespread and far-reaching. I will describe these briefly first, and then we may begin to paint.

Plate 5.—Coast Scene. Rough Sea. Study in one working.

Colours used in this Study : White, Yellow Ochre, Alizarin Crimson, and Cobalt Blue. Three colours.

Plate 6.—Moonlight. Study in two workings.

Colours used in this Study : White, Roman Ochre, Mid-Cadmium, Alizarin Crimson, Burnt Umber, and Cobalt Blue. Five colours.

Plate 7.—Sunset. Study in three workings.

Colours used in this Study : White, Pale Lemon Yellow, Yellow Ochre, Roman Ochre, Raw Sienna, Cadmium-Mid, Rose Madder, and Cobalt Blue. Seven colours.

76

Plate 8.—A Misty Morning.

Colours used in this Study : White, Lemon Yellow, Yellow Ochre, Rose Madder, and Cobalt Blue.   Four colours.

Frontispiece.—Spring : Study in three stages. No. 1, Background, first working only ; No. 2, Birch Tree, first and second workings; No. 3. Birch Tree in three workings.

Colours used in this Study : White, Pale Lemon Yellow, Yellow Ochre, Raw Sienna, Rose Madder, Raw Umber, and Cobalt Blue.   Six colours.

Plate 9.—Summer : A Devon Lane.   Study in three workings.

Colours used in this Study : White, Pale Lemon Yellow, Yellow Ochre, Raw Sienna, Alizarin Crimson, Alizarin Blue, and Cobalt Blue.   Six colours.

Plate 10. — Autumn : A Somerset Stream. Study in three workings.

Colours used in this Study : White, Yellow Ochre, Raw Sienna, Mid-Cadmium, Alizarin Crimson, Alizarin Blue, Raw Umber, Cobalt Blue. Seven Colours.

Plate 11.—Winter, a Study in two workings.

Colours used in this Study : White, Yellow Ochre, Pale Lemon Yellow, Rose Madder, Burnt Umber and Cobalt Blue.   Five colours.

The best day to choose for the painting of such subjects as those which I have drawn, is a clear

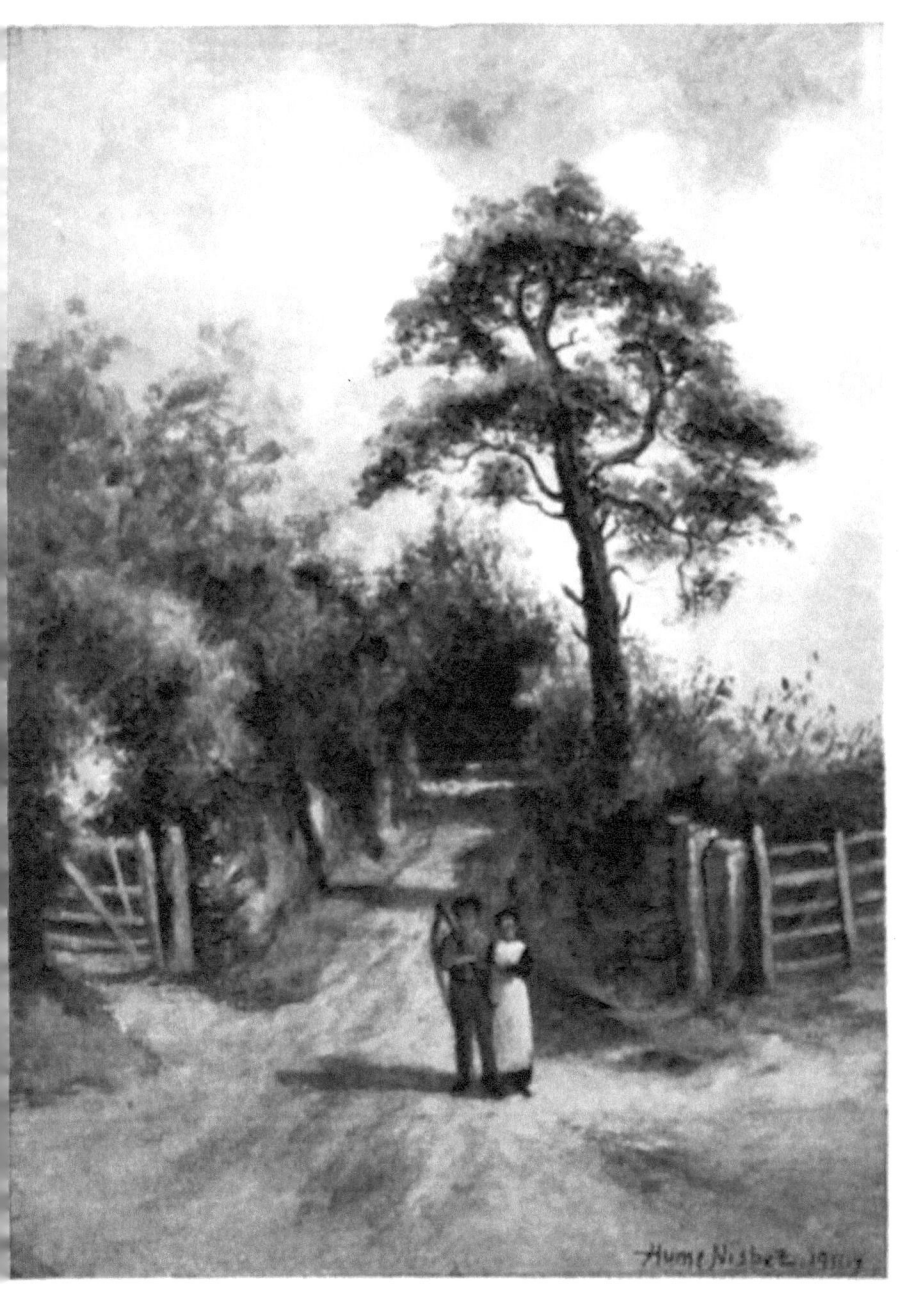

PLATE IX.—Summer—A Devon Lane.

day yet without much sunlight. You will thus be able to paint on without being disturbed by the changing of the light and altering of the effect; besides you will be able to see your local colours better.

Some painters advise the using of a small looking glass, and black convex or Claude mirror. You may do so if you like. The one will present your picture in a new aspect to you, and the other lower the general tone to an indoor kind of effect. I never use these accessories myself, as I prefer to look straight at Nature, and take it as it appears to my own vision.

One thing you must remember from the beginning. You cannot possibly copy on your canvas all that you see in the vast scale before you, so that you must make a judicious selection. This selection I advise will be the largest objects in the landscape, leaving the minor details to take care of themselves.

The palette to use in landscape painting is much the same as in Interior work, with perhaps more Yellows, and the addition of Antwerp Blue. It is not the most dependable of colours, but I cannot get on without a little of it. Of course I daresay one might get accustomed to use Viridian instead of Antwerp, and therefore it may be wiser to start with it and leave the Antwerp Blue at home. I shall try to say Viridian instead of Antwerp wherever I can do so, and you must try to do what you can with Viridian if I chance to say Antwerp. It is a great pity though that chromes and Antwerp and Prussian Blue have to be discarded, as, there is no mistake, they do produce the colours in Green that we sometimes want. This is the palette to take out with you, to cover all emergencies :—

Flake White, Lemon Yellow, Cadmium, Pale and Deep, Aureolin, Yellow and Roman Ochres, Raw Sienna, Venetian and Light Reds, Vermilion, Rose Madder or Alizarin Crimson, Raw and Burnt Umbers, Caledonian Brown, Brown Madder, Burnt Sienna, Ivory Black, Cobalt or Permanent Blue, Viridian, or the uncertain Antwerp Blue, and Sap Green.

I might add 'Naples Yellow' to these 21 colours, only, as one of its ingredients is Cadmium Sulphide, I fear that it might not altogether agree with the White Lead ; at least, when I have used Naples Yellow with Flake White the result was not quite so satisfactory, yet mixed with Terre Verte, Cobalt and Rose Madder it makes a most delicious and silvery grey ; but, as very nearly the same kind of grey can be produced by using Raw Sienna, it is useless to burden yourself with Naples Yellow.

When you have placed your canvas and easel well in the light, and have it in a position where the sun is to one side, and a little behind you, so that the full light will fall as much as possible in the same direction on your canvas as it falls upon the landscape, and have secured everything so that your canvas will not be blown over, with your paint box handy on a stone at your side, or on your camp stool (for I would advise you to stand if possible to your work)—then set your palette.

The sky and distance are what you must paint first, and the colours you require for these are :— Flake White, Lemon Yellow, a little Pale Cadmium, Yellow Ochre, Light or Venetian Red, Rose Madder, Raw Umber, Cobalt, Terre Verte, and it may be Ivory Black. Put these out and no more for the present.

Unless you strictly require the Cadmium, do not put it out, and if you do, just put out the smallest speck possible, as you will require very little of it.

I will suppose that there are some clouds in the sky with shadow sides. Begin your painting with the lightest portion of the clouds ; if they are very dazzlingly white you may add a touch of Lemon Yellow to your White, if they are soft and creamy, the Yellow Ochre will do to take the coldness from the White. Place the paint on as stiff as you can work it with your large hog-hair brush—No. 5 flat will do, if your canvas is not too big—and take plenty of paint. Lay it on massively, following the curves of the clouds, with short strokes ; in fact always follow the lines and direction of the shapes you are copying. In the first working of landscape work, also remember the advice I gave you in the figure and keep your colours subdued.

It is a daylight, forenoon or mid-day effect I am now describing. I shall have something to say afterwards about the effects of sunrise, sunset, moonlight and other atmospheric changes. Meantime there is nothing to hurry you over much.

Yet, in sky painting, you must not idle your time, for although the clouds change slowly, they are constantly altering their shape and position, and what may be white clouds when you begin, may become a spread of blue, while you are still labouring to produce the cloud. This will necessitate your exerting your memory and keeping to what you saw when you started.

Dash in the light portion of the clouds rapidly, and then round them off with their shadows. If they are light floating masses, use Cobalt and Venetian Red, or Cobalt and Rose Madder, with Yellow Ochre, varying the depths with more yellow where they are warm, or less yellow where they look purple. Terre Verte and Rose Madder will produce a nice cloud-grey Purple, and Yellow Ochre or Raw Umber added, a more decided grey or neutral tint.

Ivory Black I have learnt by experience to be a most valuable tint when used discreetly, although at one time I despised it as something unprofessional, and never carried it in my box. I fancy my black and white work taught me first to respect this formerly despised servant.

As you approach the horizon you will find that your salmon tints, yellows and purples are more decided ; put them in as you see them, more pronounced as well as deeper in tone; make shafts of colour play about the bottom of the sky, where it is nearing the earth.

Your brush will be dirty by this time. Wash it out with turpentine and wipe it clean on your rag, or take a fresh brush, for your blue—which you like, or find most convenient. Also wipe your palette, if you have covered the working part of it with the varied tints.

Near the horizon, the blue will be faint and mellow in tone. Use Yellow Ochre or Lemon Yellow with your Cobalt and Flake White to produce this mellowness, and paint the lower portions first, passing upwards by soft gradations to the deeper blues of the empyrean. Blend and soften the edges of your clouds softly, yet without too much mixing, with the blue spaces behind, and use as little medium as you can, so that your picture may not get 'smudgy' when you come to your landscape. Also see, before you leave your sky, that you have put in all the portions which shine through the leaves and branches, &c., which may be against the sky.

The greens in your distance will be very grey. Terre Verte, or Cobalt and Yellow Ochre, will produce vivid enough green for all you may require here. Greys and purples predominate. Use Yellow Ochre, Cobalt and Yellow Ochre, with perhaps Raw Umber and Ivory Black ; and to get at these, work your background as solidly as you have done your sky, and merge the edges into the sky, *i.e.*, leave no harsh or ridgy edges, yet don't make them '*woolly*,' *i.e.*, undecided ; also never under any temptation use that tool of the boarding school amateur, the ' softener.' What your hog-hair brush cannot soften leave alone till the next working.

If you have stained and dirtied your canvas with the monochrome scumbling, it will serve to show you what the key or scale of tone should be and keep you from using your colours too faintly ; yet even with the 'staining,' you will be tempted to make the distance too light and faint, particularly if it is a far spreading one. To avoid this error, keep yourself rigidly in hand and your colours down, *i.e.*, be temperate with your Flake White at this stage, and while changing the monochrome into colour, keep to the tones which that preliminary shading gave you.

In the middle distance the tints will grow more vivid as the atmosphere gets thinner, yet the Cobalt, Terre Verte and Ochre will be enough; or, if they are not, a little Raw Sienna or Lemon Yellow will give you all you require in the way of green here. The Rose Madder or Crimson still occupies a large share of the middle distance.

Look carefully after your shadows in this working, and put the broad masses in as darkly as they appear to you, leaving the darker details, of course, alone. As you are working with your hog-hair brushes, you cannot put details in, therefore never attempt to take out your sables. No. 1 flat hog-hair is the smallest brush that you will require, and what objects you cannot put in with that leave alone.

The very light portions of your picture : where sunlight falls on hill-sides or whitewashed houses or red tiles, or for the glistening of water, keep your colours low-toned ; make the glistening water and the white-washed walls a silvery grey, the red tiles a blending of Ochre and Crimson, or Venetian Red and White, subdued ; the gleaming hill-sides grey-green, or a Sienna olive tint. Never make them as bright as they appear.

My reason for this advice is, that when your picture is brought forward to the foreground you may require your bright touches then, or you may get a casual effect, *after* you have painted so far— a sudden gleam at one part of the middle distance or distance which will be the key-note of your picture. If, however, you put in all the bright places you see in the landscape as vividly as they appear, your picture, when painted in, will be a weak and confusing conglomeration of contradictory spots which you will have to tone down in order to get the proper breadth. There is no earthly use in painting what you may have to rub out, if you can help it. Light, if indiscriminately employed in detached spots, always weakens a picture. Half shadow on the other hand gives it breadth.

Your foreground is the part where you will have to exercise the most discretion and restraint. The mass of detail with which it is crowded must be rigidly kept out of sight. Do not forget that at this stage you have only to prepare the ground for what you will afterwards paint in. You have to look through all that surface tangle of weeds, leaves, bark, lichen and débris to what, if you look attentively, you will see lying beneath. Under, and through the reflections and ripples on the

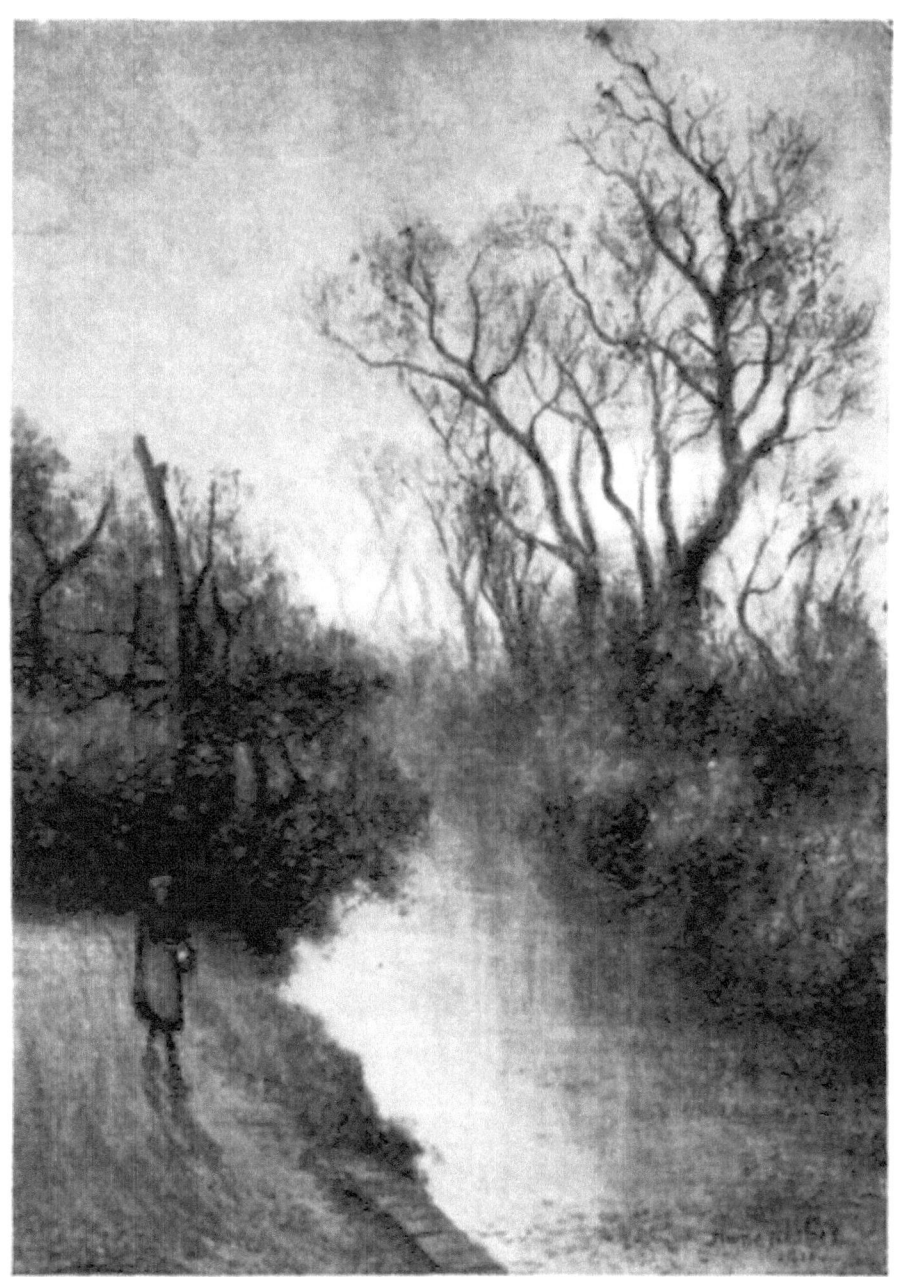

PLATE X.—Autumn—A Somerset Stream.

water, is the depth of the water itself: therefore your present duty is to paint the wealth of that under world as far as you can penetrate it, and leave the upper surface for future workings.

Bronze Greens, rich Purples and juicy Browns lie under those vividly coloured upper growths and surface reflections. If you watch carefully for a short time, it will appear to you as if some genius or wood deity had drawn back the upper covering, for your special benefit, and shown to you the underneath. That is what you have to put in to-day and no more; and, before you are done, you will find it as hard to do as you did your figure or portrait background, for it is as full of subdued richness and colour.

On the pool and river, you have nothing to do with the reflection during this working, but you must try to reproduce the transparency of the water itself. To do this you will use Raw Sienna, Sap Green, Brown Madder and, probably, Terre Verte, Rose Madder, and Cobalt. Don't be afraid of producing depth, yet try to avoid *cloudiness* and blackness. On the bank-side there are mosses, earths of various shades, roots and deep holes; to render these, use the same colours as transparently and suggestively. On the tree trunks are cracks, broken places and rich stains of all sorts besides the bark; leave the bark alone for the present, and paint the under stains and under surface. You will hardly require White at all to mix with your colours here, but plenty of Madders, Siennas, Cobalts, and Sap Greens. The under mass of foliage must be your aim, the upper leaves dismissed for the present, with the small branches. The Viridian may be used here, with a large proportion of Sienna, and transparent Brown.

You have now covered the entire surface of your canvas with suggestions, and before you take it home to dry, walk back and examine it all over. If the middle and distance do not harmonize with your low-toned and subdued foreground, try to make them do so as far as you possibly can by lowering them in gradation and giving them the proper depth, yet if you find the body colour inclined to work up and get muddled, leave it as it is for the present. You can bring it into harmony in your next working.

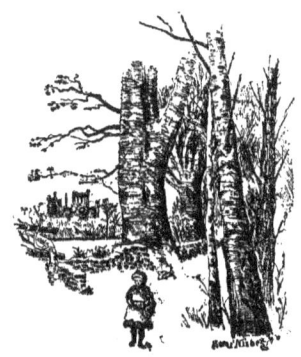

CHAPTER VIII.

SECOND WORKING :—GENERAL

HAVING shown you in the two preceding chapters the practical difference between figure and landscape painting, and as these differences are mostly observable in the first working, I shall now proceed as I did regarding the drawing out, and club the two subjects together for the rest of the space at my disposal.

I have no time in these lessons to theorize. You must find out from other works all about the theory of painting. My present aim is to tell you how to use your brushes and mix your paints ; and, as I have small enough space to tell these in, I must ignore style and be terse and abrupt in my remarks ; yet I hope that you have followed me so far easily, and that you will find my remarks lucid enough for you to work from, right from the beginning to the end.

Your picture is now perfectly dry, and you must be sure about this point before you begin your second working; indeed, the paint ought to be hard, not only on the surface but underneath as well, before you touch it again—particularly so if you have to scrape any of it off. As I like to load my own canvases heavily with colours, I generally begin a considerable number and set them aside for months, sometimes for years, before I touch them again; but then I always make careful sketches, so that I may not forget my subject and effect. Likewise I work my canvas, when possible, from Nature direct. I also make copious notes of descriptive matter about each subject in my private notebook, after I have done my first working.

However, as every one may not possess my tenacity of memory and dogged patience, also, as the seasons will not wait your time, while the models will inevitably grow older, you must be content to have your colours as dry as possible in the time at your disposal; only be sure that the surface is thoroughly dry, so that it may stand a good hard rub, before you take up your canvas again. Some colours are slower driers than others. Rose Madder, Raw Sienna, and most of the transparent colours are slow in drying, Vandyke Brown particularly so. Test those places where these colours are laid on purely, by touching them lightly with your finger before you begin. If they are hard, you may be satisfied that the rest of the canvas is also ready for your second working.

Begin by sponging your picture over with cold water and drying it with a soft and worn but clean cotton rag. My old shirts come in handy for paint rags. This ablution serves two purposes: it removes all exuding oils, dust, and dirt; and it makes the oil with which you have to rub it over lie smoothly upon the surface.

Having washed and dried the canvas, dip a piece of rag in linseed, poppy or nut oil and rub that all over the surface, drying it off again as clean as you can; this also serves two purposes, to freshen the dry paint, and to enable the colours in your second working to lie on, blend and amalgamate with the colours underneath. Often, where the colours look flat and dull, this rubbing of oil will bring back the appearance which they had when they were first painted, and so save you the trouble of re-touching them.

One point I wish you to keep always in your mind. If your colour is all right in the first working, there can be no possible advantage in re-painting it, but rather a positive injury. The finishing of a picture does not mean painting it solidly over and over a certain number of times. Finishing means, adding to the value, and harmonizing the colours which are already on your canvas, and there are always qualities of purity and clearness in your first painting which, if you don't take the greatest care will be lost in your second and succeeding workings. Bear this constantly in your mind, and you will work with judgment and deliberation.

Set up your canvas. Also set your palette with a full complement of colours ; you can put out all your colours for this working, as you may require them. You may also have to use all your brushes ; only begin with the largest hog-hairs first, and as you proceed you can take up the smaller brushes down to the finest sable ; only do not use your sables where the hog-hair will do as well.

The first consideration is the harmonizing of the different parts of your picture : look after all detached, glaring and spotty parts, and bring them into keeping with the rest. This must be your preliminary work, so that you may not be disturbed in your mind when painting the details, as you will then have your tones or scale complete. To do this, you will use '*glazings*,' *i.e.*, transparent colours, to tone down your foreground, and '*scumblings,*' *i.e.*, the mixture of opaque colours, to tone down your distances and middle distances.

All unnecessary roughnesses you had better scrape away before you wash and oil your canvas.

The next consideration is, your effects of light. Decide at once, and for ever, on this important matter, and do not chop about, or change afterwards. Be also chary with your light ; a picture ought, to be effective, to be single in this respect, and as a rule it can only afford to carry one high light and that in a very small proportion, with all the other lights graduating in more subdued or secondary tones. Of course there is no hard or fast law about this, therefore you must use your own good taste and judgment. When you have harmonized your masses and chosen your high lights you had better let your canvas dry again before proceeding farther.

Once more wash, oil and wipe dry, and then commence with your details. This part of the work may occupy a considerable time and many days' working ; the best plan is to devote yourself to a small portion of the canvas and do that thoroughly before taking up the next part to it.

Go over your canvas bit by bit, and do not jump from one end to the other. Also all the time you are filling in the details keep studying the general harmony of the whole. Do not elaborate one part to the damage of the other.

In painting the details you must try to produce these as much as possible by suggestions, and with as few lines as possible. The hair on the eyebrows and eyelashes is composed of a multitude of lines, or single hairs, we all know, but you must rather give the impression of these hairs by suggestive blendings of light and dark than make them photographically hard and stiff, and the hog-hair flat brush No. 4 will do this more successfully than the finest "rigger" or writing pencil. The beard and head hair must also be rendered in the same way, by paying strict attention to the masses of light and shadow.

The flesh tints must be worked over until they appear as in the model, peach-like where the down comes, clear where the skin is bare, transparent in such thin portions as the nostrils and ears. The shadow also will have to be blended with the lights to produce the proper softness and round-ness; yet take care while you aim at getting the softness, shine and transparency, that you do not

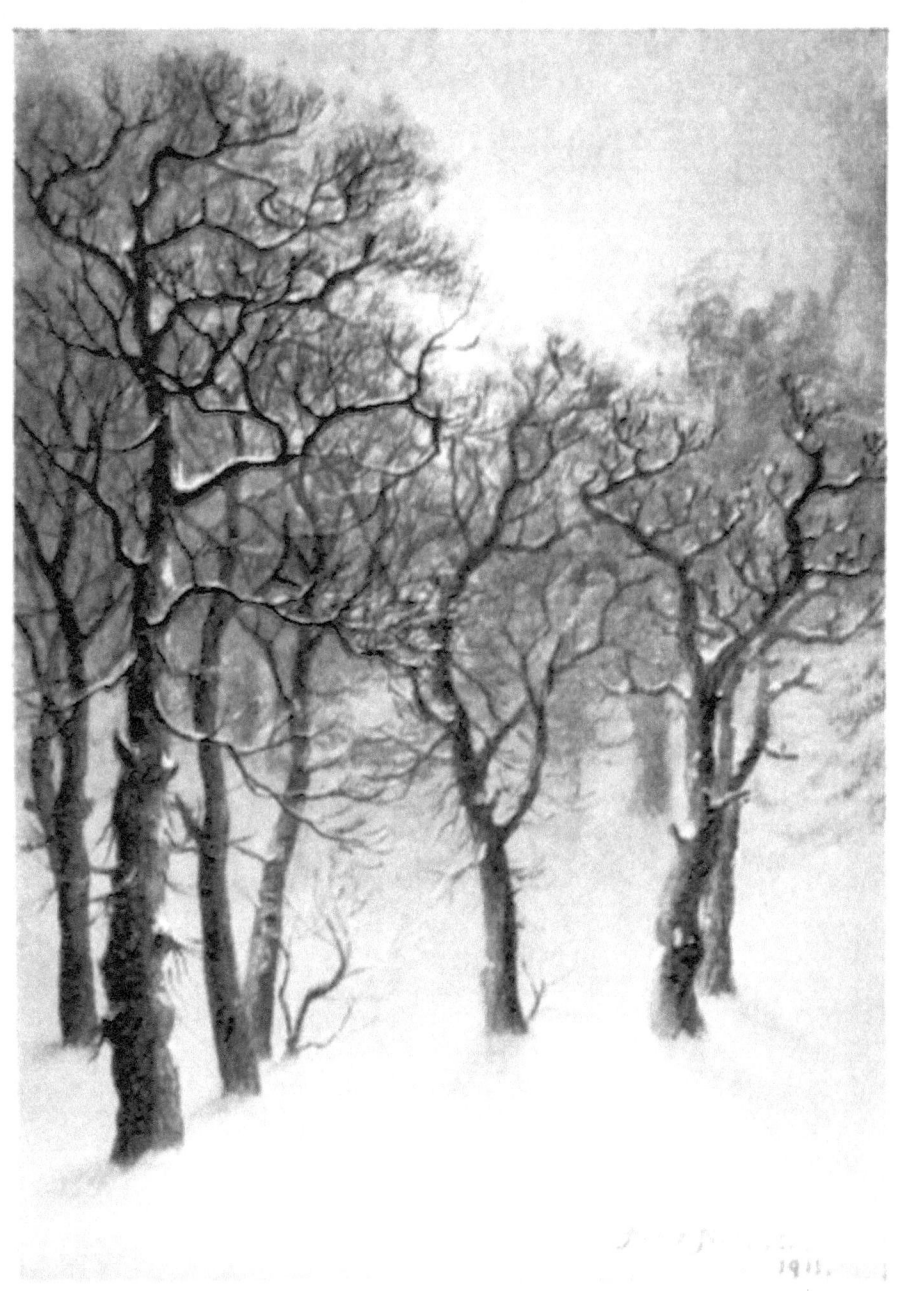

1915.

PLATE XI.—Winter.

make your work waxy or opaque, *i.e.*, you must help, and not hide, your first clear and pure working. The effect of paint laid over paint, if not laid properly, is to render it hard, muddy and solid. To lay it on properly, you must keep to the variety of tones which you placed first, in the same subtle order, and, while painting softer, never cover over a large space hurriedly or carelessly.

The touches of light where they fall will now be all put in, with the folds and wrinkles.

The details of houses, &c., the barks on the trunks, with the leaves, weeds and grasses which overgrow the undergrowth will now be added, one growth overlapping the other by suggestive touches rather than lines or dots. The uppermost leaves may be touched in at places, by definite touches; yet even here you must not exaggerate Nature, for, if you mentally reduce the size of the nearest leaf to the size of your picture, it will be doubtful if you have a brush small enough to put it in. Therefore as you cannot do this and keep to the same proportion of your original, do what you can, which is, suggest them by artful cross workings, and hatchings. A photograph will show the leaves nearest *in dots*, but, as you can easily prove, if you push forward your hand or your foot, when getting your likeness taken, the camera always exaggerates the objects that are nearest to the lens.

Where nothing else except lines can be seen, such as in the smaller branches and roots of trees, the masts, yards and shrouds of ships, use then your sables and "riggers"; yet you will not find a single line throughout your subject that is not broken up by a variety of tones and colours; therefore every line and cord must be gone over many times with different tints and shades before it will be exactly like the line before you.

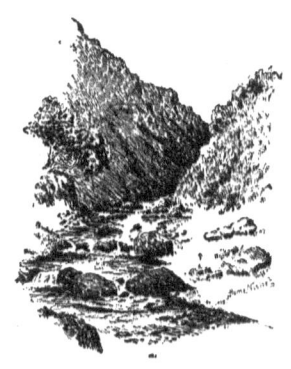

CHAPTER IX.

FINISHING THE PICTURE.

YOUR picture is now done, as far as the detail, the rounding, the drawing and the likeness are concerned, but as you have been working over it in a patchy and detached manner it will require to be brought together again and the whole re-united. It will also want depth, transparency and richness. To do this is the final and most delicate process, the portion over which you must linger tenderly and do a great deal more watching than actual working.

It is best to set the picture away for a time until you have almost forgotten it, then take it up and look at it with a fresh eye. You will not run the risk then of giving it work which it does not want.

Possibly a rub over with medium and a very thin glazing in shadow parts, or a little toning down or brightening up will be all that is needed to complete it.

As you watch it, you think, perhaps, that a little more atmosphere in the distance will improve it, something to throw back for a few yards a hill or a house; a tree trunk or a shadow may be too dark and strong. They are asserting themselves

too much for the general unity ; a slight '*scumble*'
of the White, Cobalt and Raw Sienna will produce
the haze you need.

The water needs an extra ripple, or the ripples
are too hard. The reflections want juiciness or
transparency. A glaze of Sap Green, or Raw
Sienna and Brown Madder, or Caledonian will
remedy this.

A shadow is too hot or too cold, a little Cobalt
or Black will cool it, or a little Raw Sienna and
Brown Madder will warm it, as the case may be.

The '*scumblings*' must be put on pretty dry,
rubbed in hard with the hog-hair, and wiped with
the rag, or your finger, to reduce their density.
The '*glazings*' are put in mostly like varnishes,
with Copal Varnish thinned with turpentine, or
with medium.

One touch, or tone, in one part will lead you on
to an improving touch or tone in some other
part. These when they are dry may have to be
re-glazed or re-scumbled and touched again.
Indeed this period may be finished by a wipe of
medium, or continued for many days. It is very
delicate and exhausting work, this finishing ; for
although you may only put half a dozen of touches
per day to your picture, your critical powers,
observing and discriminating faculties, are on the
stretch all the time.

Never attempt to finish your picture unless you are very fresh and in first-class working form, and when you feel wearied give it up, or you may spoil all your former good work by a maladroit touch, a dirty or clumsy glaze.

Approach your picture also in a confident and hopeful mood. If you have worked on it long, the after effects will likely be dejection and diffidence, for after the strain, the bow is unbent, *i.e.*, the mind becomes passive and listless; let this mood pass which makes you fancy you have perpetrated a failure. Keep from looking at it for a time, until you recover your normal mood; take a change, and then when you next look at it you may find that you have not done so badly after all.

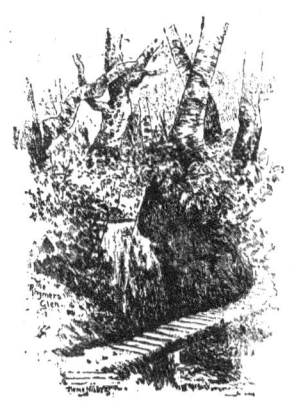

H

CHAPTER X.

TEMPERA PAINTING.

WHEN the artist or student begins this most fascinating and satisfactory process of painting he will at once comprehend the unconscious want that the discovery of it supplies. It is an advance in material, convenience and utility, as far as technique and easy manipulation of colours, effect and rapid finish in out-door work are to be regarded ; as incandescent gas-light has been to the candles of Queen Anne's nights, or motor-cars to stage coaches.

The advantages of Tempera colours are manifold over either oil or water colour : when working from Nature—catching rapid effects of light and shade, the swift motion of waves and clouds, for-ever changing in form and colour ; when planning out imaginative studies, or depicting action of any kind in the air, the sea, the land, humanity or animal life ; for they can be worked under conditions which would be impossible for the using of either oil or water colours.

They work like butter, when the temperature is

at 60 degrees, *i.e.*, neither too stiff nor too soft they fix almost instantly, without leaving hardness anywhere whether the artist is sketching a winter scene, or a tempest of wind, snow, or rain. If he can endure the weather, the Tempera will not fail him, but from start to finish will look under each touch like the softest of velvet.

There are no uncertainties about this mode of working, as in oils, water colours, or the dry pastels; each brush-touch is a definite step, which is revocable at will, or ultimate, if the worker is satisfied with what he has done. To the student who has not yet mastered the technical difficulties of oil or water colour painting, this will come with an ease that is surprising, but, to the adept in either mode it will be a delight and a revelation of how much effort and time may be saved from slow manipulation for the development of thought.

Another advantage is, that it may be used on almost any surface or material without any preparation—on canvas primed or natural, on wood, paper, silk or linen ; and, perhaps not the least of its advantages, the brushes are as easily washed with water after use, as if they had been used in distemper. This to a sketcher, when tired out with a day's work in the open, is no small comfort.

These new colours are of the Impasto or

H 2

Tempera order, but dry like oil paint and will not wash off when they are *quite dry* if the medium prepared for their use is used with them.

This medium is largely composed of eggs—the yolk as well as the white. These possibly were used by the ancient Egyptians and Greeks in their Fresco work. No other varnish nor fixitive dries so hard, tough or hermetical as the glutinous contents of an egg; and I wish to say a few words about some of its uses and qualities, to show that no other medium can equal the enduring qualities of this, as I have proved by long experience and numerous tests.

The white of a raw egg beaten up, makes the best size to coat over gilding, bronze work, or gold paint; the objection gilders have to its use is that it cannot be removed by any ordinary process when the frame requires re-gilding; it is imperishable in itself, and insoluble in water, ether, spirits or turpentine. It is also more hermetic than glass, or any other varnish or glaze, therefore it protects from the injurious effects of the atmosphere whatever is under it. This sealing in, or preserving quality makes the contents of the egg the most valuable adjunct or medium that an artist, who wishes his colours to endure as he has left them, could possibly use to paint with, to

have his paints ground with, and to varnish over
after his picture is finished, either in water colour
or oil painting.

Although infinitely closer in its texture than
any varnish, it never becomes brittle as all
gummy varnishes and sizes do become when
they dry hard. It is always tenacious and
elastic in its texture and adherence ; hence its
use as a mender for broken glass or china, and
more especially with articles that are unglazed.
It can be folded, *i.e.*, silk, paper, parchment, or other
fabrics may be folded, when coated over with this
egg medium, without cracking in the slightest
degree, no matter how many years may have
elapsed since it has been used, as it stretches like
india-rubber. This I have proved as I used it, in
silk and velvet-painting, instead of size, gum or oil,
many years ago, and tested its qualities undei tropic
suns. Of course, through my not having the advantage
of a scientific and chemical education, the mixtures
I made had many defects, which are now obviated
and corrected by the chemical knowledge and
experience of such experts as Messrs. Reeves and
Sons have at their command in their old-established
laboratory, which I had blindly to guess at in my
ignorance ; but I was successful enough in my
past efforts to be able to appreciate the greatness
and future possibilities of this new and successful

discovery ; a discovery which I am of opinion will be an artistic revolution, rather than an advance or new branch. To put it plainly, I am of strong conviction since I have tried these new colours, and medium, that the days of oil painting, at least, are numbered, and that Tempera will take its place, as soon as artists get used to it.

Water colours may endure longer, yet as I find it can be used in the same ways, *i.e.,* either as pure washes or in impasto, I cannot see that artists will long trouble to carry two colour boxes to the country when one can serve for both modes of expression. I will admit that I have my prejudices still in favour of the old systems for certain work, but this may be that I have not yet mastered more than the rudiments of the possibilities of Tempera technique, and I therefore write under correction.

Par example. I think for large studio subjects and canvases that oil paints or, perhaps, the first and second workings in Tempera, and the after finishing in oils, may be preferred with painters who, like myself, have been long addicted to oil colours and large brushes, and that this adroit blending of the two modes will be of immense help both in time, labour and invention. If this plan is adopted, the Tempera canvases must be used, or some preparation of zinc white and egg

medium used to prepare and alter the surface
of canvases already prepared for oil painting.
They must be to some extent made absorbent,
as I find Tempera colours do not *set* fast enough
on an oil-painted ground. But this difficulty is
easy to get over, as all artists know, with a wash
of distemper. Doubtless the inventors will meet
this difficulty with some proper preparation to
suit Tempera.

In pure water-colour I have found no difficulty
in getting exactly the same effects with Tempera
colours, using water freely in the first wash,
as I have already suggested in my book " On
Painting in Water Colours." Do not be tempted
to use white in this moist and transparent system,
that is all. The colours work the same, with this
added advantage, that you will know when your
work is thoroughly hard dry, which it will be
in a week. It will not wash off, and also the
atmosphere and light will not affect it at all.
It is hermetically sealed. This brings me to
the point where ordinary water colours will stil
hold their own, or rather that an adroit blending
of Tempera and water colours, reversing the
order of working, will be of invaluable advantage.
In oil painting you may begin your work with
Tempera colours, but you cannot finish with them
over oil work. Indeed, there would be no advantage

to be gained in doing this that I can as yet see, although I see many advantages in beginning a large oil painting in Tempera. But when done, and the painting, *i.e.*, the surface, is thoroughly dry, the colours will certainly endure longer if covered with an egg varnish instead of an oil or gum varnish. But the oil must be dried out of the colours used first, and that will take about a couple of years, or longer, if not exposed to a strong light and a dry atmosphere.

Sir G. F. Watts wrote to me that his system was to expose his pictures during each working for months in a glass-house, where they baked in the sunlight, and, after they were finished, for at least six months, before varnishing them. Many of his pictures occupied years in the painting, as he set them aside when tired and only took them up when in the mood, having numerous canvases on hand, all drying in this fashion, while they waited. This, I think, is the proper mode to produce a mature work, as it is to procure a lasting picture as far as the colours are concerned. Had this truly great master lived to see the advent of Tempera colours I am positive he would have been an early convert. Certainly he would have discarded all forms of oil and gum varnishes in favour of egg medium to cover his finished and properly dried masterpieces.

The oil must be thoroughly out of the colours
before the atmosphere is excluded, or it will
destroy their purity and blacken them. As
ordinary varnish is porous to a certain extent
the oil can exude and form a film, which should
be wiped and washed away at intervals. This
should also be done with an unvarnished oil
painting, while drying, until the colours are almost
in the condition of adhesive powder. It is then
quite dry, and, if coated first with the egg medium,
it can be varnished with impunity with mastic
varnish and may be depended to last as long
as the canvas, with *no* change nor alteration of
the colours. A pure water-colour painting where
no Chinese white is employed, and where the
artist likes to linger over wiping out and refining,
which also may occupy months in the working,
must be done—until the finishing washes and
touches—with water colours and not Tempera.
But the final washes can be used with Tempera
colours and diluted egg medium, and a final wash
over will lock up the colours and make them
fadeless ; and also, if the back of the paper is
coated as well with this medium, it will be quite
impervious to damp : this without in the slightest
degree interfering with the delicacy of the drawing.
For all rapid sketching, whether impasto or transparent, Tempera colours are the best to use instead of

oil or water colours. I cannot, on the score of
health, recommend the use of either dry pastels
or oil pastels. Cases of poisoning have been
known from the use of the oil pastels, and
the dry pastels are only a little less dangerous.
But the Tempera colours are put up in tubes and
used in the same way as oil and water colours,
with brushes or palette knife, and are safe to
the worker. Hog-hairs, Lyons bristles, and
Ichneumon hair brushes are most suitable,
and the longer the hair the better. For sizes,
Nos. 1, 3, 6, 8, and 12, Ichneumon I have
found handy for general small work, but this the
student must decide for himself. One parting
advice :—lay the colours on full and lightly
and don't scrub, and you will produce beautiful
and satisfactory work in this new style of
painting.

The Frontispiece — " Spring—Study in three
stages "—will serve as an excellent example of
what can be done with Tempera in one sitting.

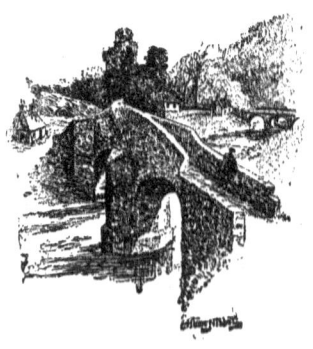

CHAPTER XI.

CONCLUDING REMARKS.

I AM almost at the end, not of my subject, but of my space; and, although I trust that I have given you some useful hints so that you may go on, by yourselves, and do some good and true work, there are a great number of branches which it is impossible for me to enter upon as I should like, in this short treatise. However, I shall try to anticipate and answer briefly a few of the many thoughts which I have no doubt will spring to being in the minds of my readers.

I have written about Figure painting and Landscape, but I have told you nothing about Seascapes and Ships ; nothing about Flower or Fruit painting, or those fugitive and yet splendid aerial and atmospheric effects which Turner painted so grandly and Ruskin has written about so poetically. Permit me to take all these subjects in rotation and deal with them in a summary manner, since I have no room left to enter, at length, upon them.

Seascape, Ships and Boats, &c. The same rules which apply to Landscape apply to the painting of the ocean and all that traverse its surface or nestle along its shores—with this difference, that, whereas the Landscape is less liable to very quick changes, the fickle Ocean is hardly ever for one hour in the same mood ; therefore you must be more rapid in your actions, and depend more upon your memory as well as your sketch book and quick sketches. It is much better to begin with Landscape than Seascape for this reason.

To achieve anything like success a Sea-painter must fill his sketch book with pencil notes and tinted sketches of sky and water effects, ships, fishing boats, fishermen afloat and ashore, all the thousand quaint and picturesque accessories which he cannot fail to come upon at any sea-board. A few water colours will be necessary to tint his drawings where necessary. Cobalt, Ochre, Raw Sienna, Crimson, Warm Sepia and Black will be enough for this purpose.

He ought likewise to make as many oil sketches as he possibly can. Indeed, while he is painting his picture, he should have a few pochade panels beside him, so that he may dash in the passing effects, for future, if not present use. Water colour sketches are not so useful as oil sketches for a painter in oils, as the treatment is so different. A Lawrence Phillips' sketching palette with frame attached for panels $11\frac{1}{2}$ by $8\frac{1}{2}$, or $8\frac{1}{2}$ by 5 in., is useful for this kind of work, as you can put a number of small impressions on each panel and carry two wet ones with safety.

Unless you can get under shelter, you will have to trust to your memory in the painting of a storm ; and even under shelter you may rub in a picture roughly, but you can never expect the same kind of storm twice. Your sketch block comes in handy here, as you will find it necessary to make several rapid sketches before you can grip the form of one wave or the upward toss of the spray.

The safest picture to attempt is the reproduction of a grey sea and cloudy sky with the surf rolling in upon the sands, as these effects are not so uncommon ; also you will be able to observe the colours of the sea and the advancing breakers. Be sparing with your accessories, and, if you can get the deliciously fresh and varied silvery tones which are round you, be content with these. The palette for an effect of this kind will be, Flake White, Lemon Yellow, Yellow Ochre, Raw Sienna, Venetian Red, Rose Madder, Raw Umber, Terre Verte, Cobalt and Black. The grey of the distance will be Yellow Ochre, Rose Madder and Cobalt, the mid-distance Raw Sienna instead of the Yellow Ochre ; the foreground grey, Terre Verte, Lemon Yellow, Raw Sienna and Rose Madder combined in varying degrees. Paint rapidly, and with loaded brushes, for you are painting rapid motion and heaving masses ; use your palette knife as well as your brush to lay on the paint, and surf, and if your palette knife works too hard dabble about with your fingers ; I don't know any finer sea brush than the point of one's forefinger. Watch keenly, while you paint quickly, for the variations are ten times more subtle and difficult to catch than the play of colours over a landscape.

Flower and Fruit Painting. You will have more time given to you in painting fruit, as it keeps longer fresh, but flowers must be done definitely and at once, while the first bloom is on them, and before they begin to blow or fade. Have your palette and canvas ready and your picture arranged in your mind and partly sketched out before you cut the flowers ; then do not waste too much time arranging them but dash into the painting at once. The best flower painting is done in one working, although you may glaze a little afterwards, from memory, to make them more dewy, moist and vivid. I would advise the judicious use of a little copal varnish for this quick work as your medium, particularly if you have to use much Rose Madder, as in Roses.

The flowers or fruit will give you the suggestion for the colours you have to use, as these are generally pretty positive. Begin by rubbing in your ground, also the part of your background next the flowers, with the different tints several tones lower than are the colours of the flowers you design to reproduce, and paint your ground work without white and transparent. If they are red or crimson roses, use at first Rose Madder with a little varnish purely, and shade it with Brown Madder. For Yellow, use Raw Sienna shaded with Burnt Sienna and Raw Umber. For Blue, Cobalt shaded with Ultramarine, for Purple, these with the addition of Rose Madder. For the green-leaves, use Sap Green, Terre Verte, Raw Sienna and Burnt Umber.

Divide the petals, and form the general shapes, with your shadow-tints, leaving the canvas with the heavy glaze over it as your present highest lights; do as much as you can with these transparent glazes until they begin to set, or grow sticky, then work your mixture of white and local colouring as dry and plentiful as you can load them on. As this body colour sets, glaze over it lightly with a long and thin hog-hair, the Rose Madder or other colours laid on purely, producing in this way your under petals. If the flower is pure scarlet, as a geranium, paint it in with Pale Vermilion, and glaze over with Rose Madder. Work up by solid colour and then glaze, fleck each colour on so lightly that you do not disturb the colour beneath, and brush over them as soon as they are stiff enough with the glazing. By this method if you manage not to mix up the colours, which you can only accomplish by practice, you will produce glowing and natural flowers. The accessories and main portion of the background you can paint after the flowers are done, provided you have shaded the portion next the flowers deep enough to make them stand out where needful, and melt into it in the shadow.

Of course you can paint flowers in a careful and deliberate fashion which will be good enough from a decorative point, yet it is almost impossible to keep them from looking like wax or artificial flowers, if painted in successive layers. If you want the dew upon the flowers, and as they appear when first cut, you must paint them from the beginning to end before the colours have time to dry. As they dry, they will soften gently into each other and always appear moist and fresh.

Aerial and Atmospheric Effects. It is impossible to get past Turner when we attempt to paint air and sky pictures, and those who live in London have the same effects nearly every day that inspired that wonderful genius. The smokes, fogs and fumes of this great City produce exquisite skies for colour and the most mysterious

effects in the world. Take your stand on any of
the Bridges below Westminster, at Dawn, Sunrise,
Mid-day, Sunset or Midnight, either Winter,
Spring, Summer or Autumn, and you will seldom
be disappointed in the glorious panorama which
spreads before your eyes.

In the dawn the grey mists are hanging over
the city, the river and the opalesque space above ;
russet-sailed barges glide upon the silvery river
from pearly mists ; mysterious shapes, which are
buildings, loom grandly on each side. There are
the colours of the prismatic oyster shell on every
side of us in this peaceful and dewy hour before
the sun appears—yellow, crimson, purple green.
In the oyster shell these direct colour shafts are
most apparent, and have shine and lustre, while
except upon the surface of the Thames, the direct
colour shafts are subtler and more intricate ; that is
all the difference. The sun rises, and the tender
mists become clouds, still fully charged with cool
and prismatic tints, the blues and purples become
more pronounced in the shadow, while, where the
clouds are thin and the light is bursting through,
the yellows and reds predominate. To see how
much distinct and separate colour there is in a
sunrise, look at its reflection in a darkened window
pane or a still pool of water. Your first working
of this effect had better be done as you see it in

the dark glass or the pool. Afterwards you can soften it by 'scumblings' of White, Yellow Ochre, Rose Madder, Cobalt and Terre Verte.

Mid-day effects, when the bright sunlight is on them, are harder and crisper in their working; the shadows also are bluish, particularly at the edges where the shadow meets with the sun glare. Of course through all this blue tone the local colour must be put in also, and likewise where the sunlight falls on roofs, &c., the local tints are definite, if in a light key. Glass, when placed flat or slanting on a roof, reflects the sky like a still pool, or the glare of the sun.

Sunsets are like sunrises, only dryer, more glowing and gorgeous, and less prismatic in their character. The reason for this is, I suppose, that there is not so much mist and moisture about them, the clouds are more gaseous than vapoury, therefore the tints glitter metallically rather than gleam prismatically. Lemon Yellow is the brightest yellow of the morning and Rose Madder the most decided crimson. Cadmiums, pale and deep, take the place of the morning yellow, in sunsets, and Vermilion comes into the glowing reds of the evening.

These effects must all be painted rapidly and sketchily in the first place, and painted afterwards more elaborately from the sketches and memory.

There can be no dawdling over these first sketches, or *impressions*, as your original is changing both form and colour every second. The brushes must fly over the pochade panel with swift and sure sweeps. The centre of light always first, then the next degrees of tone and so on, from the sun to the shadows; by this system you keep your brushes and palette clean as long as you need pure colours and strong lights.

Moonlight and night effects must be done entirely from rough pencil or charcoal strokes and memory. Charcoal is the best to make your notes with, or pastels. Pick out a Yellow Ochre tinted crayon, a Light Red one, a Blue and a Brown crayon, and place them where you can get at them by touch, for you will not see them very well, and you may get something of the effect of colour that way to make your sketch.

If it is a moist moon-rise you may have all the colour of a sunset in more subdued tones; but moonlights are generally pearly, silvery grey, or greenish and mellow. The effect of brightness, depth and hazy mystery, you can only get by successive workings, scumblings and glazings. The shadows of moonlight are generally warm brown.

Storms on sea and land vary in their colour and position and require to be robustly painted.

Thick colour is the best for them, and bold large brush work. The storm effect on the title page may guide you somewhat as to the kind of work required. The palette which I used in my painting of this picture contained Flake White, Yellow Ochre, Raw Sienna, Light Red (or Venetian Red), Crimson, Cobalt, Terre Verte and Black.

Water Reflections, &c. A still pool is perhaps the easiest of all kinds of water surface to paint, although it requires a great deal of attention and close work. As I have described in my first and future workings of foregrounds, you will paint it from the bottom upwards, *i.e.*, the colour of the depth first and then the objects which are mirrored upon that depth. Every object that lies above must be repeated, only in a softer and more liquid manner, the details trailing and melting into one another. Moving or rushing water must be painted quickly, and before you put your brush on your canvas, you must have learnt, by close watching, all the tricks, swirls, colours and shapes of the ripples, rapids, or waves as they leap, twist and fall. The foam portions are always put on lastly.

Animal Painting. Very few artists succeed in this branch, and the practice of it requires a vast amount of patience and even temper. If you do not love animals you will never succeed in painting them. They are restless and bad models, so that you must follow them about and take dozens of sketches of each study, before you dare hope to make one portrait. Dogs and cats, being more domesticated, sit best. 'Landseer' and 'Morland' are two good masters to copy as specimens of different styles of work.

Impressionism. Before you attempt to take impressionist pictures you must learn to paint as I have told you in previous chapters, for no style of work exhibits the ignorance of a painter more than this, and what in the hands of a master is the true effect of a first glance, will be an impudent and meaningless daub of crudeness in the hands of an amateur. When the eye first falls upon an object, what it sees is a mass of colour with only vague form. The form comes out after the colour is grasped, and as the Impressionists *justly* contend, that first glance is the only true one, because Nature changes every second of time; therefore what you see after looking for some moments, is not exactly what you saw at first.

It is therefore impossible to elaborate this phase of Nature. You must look at it with a single eye and paint it positively and even crudely as well as vaguely. At the best, however, this style of painting can only be classed with sketches, therefore I cannot recommend it to a beginner, although as a painter I endorse its stern truth.

Some painters, Gainsborough amongst others, recommend the beginning of a picture in candle or lamplight. You will get stronger and deeper effects of light and shade by an artificial light, yet you must always finish your picture in daytime if you should try this experiment—as an experiment only.

Looking at the masterpieces of that late genius, G. F. Watts, one can see that he depends upon no mannerism or style for the creation of his effects, as every picture has an original method of its own and seems to be purely an experiment to suit the individual subject. It is *by work* that he has achieved his successful results, and I daresay it would be impossible for him to describe his blendings. He has studied his subjects to the core, and appears to be careless as to the pigments he uses, or the treatment he gives them in building up and finishing. This of course is how a true genius works, as a student of Nature all his life.

My last advice is : Paint naturally, and be ruthless in your search after Truth. Never attempt to flatter, or paint excuses for Nature. Try to follow modestly, yet doggedly, where she leads, and to copy exactly what she reveals to you ; for, depend upon it, what you may regard as blunders will always be a thousand times better than your foolish and audacious attempts to disguise or improve.

I think I have now played the rôle of Teacher quite enough for the present. You must try to do the rest for yourselves as far as Oil Painting is concerned. I may tell you how to begin painting in water colour at some future time, and as I retire permit me to wish you God-speed in your efforts after the Beautiful and the True. Court Nature assiduously, and she will not disappoint you.

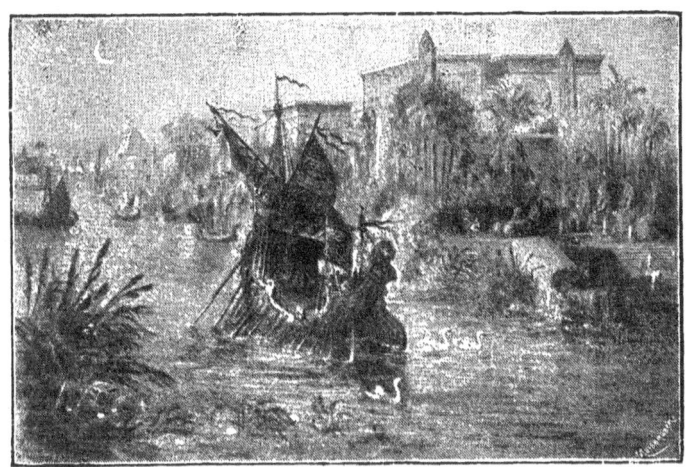

INDEX.

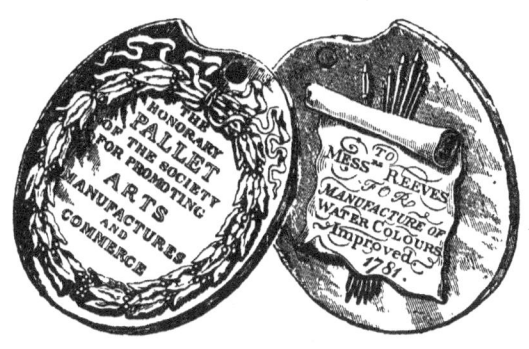

THE SILVER PALETTE ABOVE WAS PRESENTED TO REEVES
AND SONS IN 1781 BY THE SOCIETY OF ARTS OF LONDON
FOR THEIR SERVICES TO ART. REEVES AND SONS' ARTISTS'
COLOURS HAVE BEEN USED BY THE LEADING ARTISTS FOR
166 YEARS. TESTIMONIALS TO THE EXCELLENCE OF
REEVES' COLOURS ARE IN EXISTENCE, RANGING FROM DAVID
COX, LEITCH, SAMUEL PROUT, ETTY, WILLIAM HUNT, ETC.,
TO THE ROYAL ACADEMICIANS OF TO-DAY.

C. NAPIER HEMY, A.R.A., recently wrote of Reeves'
colours after contrasting them with four other makers'
colours previously used by him :—

"I found yours a deeper, richer set of colours than I had
ever found before, both in oil and water colour. I really
consider they are the very best I have ever had."

———◆———

REEVES' COLOURS ARE TO BE OBTAINED AT ANY DEALERS, BUT ONLY THOSE WITH THE "GREYHOUND" TRADE MARK ARE THEIR ARTISTS' QUALITY.

REEVES' ARTISTS' OIL COLOURS.

Size of Tube No.	2	3	4	4A	8	12	24
	s. d.	s. d.	s. d.	s. d.	s. d.	s. d.	s. d.
Alizarin Blue .. EACH	0 4½	—	—	0 7½	1 0	1 4	2 6
Alizarin Brown Madder .. ,,	0 4½	—	—	0 7½	1 0	1 4	2 6
Alizarin Crimson ,,	0 4½	—	—	0 7½	1 0	1 4	2 6
Alizarin Green Pale ,,	0 4½	—	—	0 7½	1 0	1 4	2 6
Alizarin Green Middle ,,	0 4½	—	—	0 7½	1 0	1 4	2 6
Alizarin Green Deep ,,	0 4½	—	—	0 7½	1 0	1 4	2 6
Alizarin Orange.. ,,	0 4½	—	—	0 7½	1 0	1 4	2 6
Alizarin Purple Lake ,,	0 4½	—	—	0 7½	1 0	1 4	2 6
Alizarin Purple Madder .. ,,	0 4½	—	—	0 7½	1 0	1 4	2 6
Alizarin Scarlet Madder .. ,,	0 4½	—	—	0 7½	1 0	1 4	2 6
Alizarin Yellow .. ,,	0 4½	—	—	0 7½	1 0	1 4	2 6
Antwerp Blue .. ,,	—	0 4½	—	—	0 10½	1 2	2 3
Aureolin .. ,,	1 6	—	—	2 9	5 0	7 0	13 0
Azo Orange .. ,,	0 6	—	—	0 10	1 6	2 0	3 6
Azo Red .. ,,	0 6	—	—	0 10	1 6	2 0	3 6
Azo Violet .. ,,	0 10½	—	—	1 6	2 9	4 0	7 6
Azo Yellow .. ,,	0 6	—	—	0 10	1 6	2 0	3 6
Bitumeff .. ,,	—	—	0 4½	—	0 7½	0 10	1 6
Blue Black .. ,,	—	0 4½	—	—	0 10½	1 2	2 3
Brown Pink .. ,,	0 4½	—	—	0 7½	1 0	1 4	2 6
Brown Madder .. ,,	0 6	—	—	0 10	1 6	2 0	3 6
Burnt Sienna .. ,,	—	—	0 4½	—	0 7½	0 10	1 6
Burnt Umber .. ,,	—	—	0 4½	—	0 7½	0 10	1 6
Cadmium Ex. Pale ,,	1 6	—	—	2 9	5 0	7 0	13 0
Cadmium Pale .. ,,	1 6	—	—	2 9	5 0	7 0	13 0
Cadmium Middle ,,	1 6	—	—	2 9	5 0	7 0	13 0
Cadmium Deep .. ,,	1 6	—	—	2 9	5 0	7 0	13 0
Cadmium Red .. ,,	1 6	—	—	2 9	5 0	7 0	13 0
Cadmium Scarlet ,,	1 6	—	—	2 9	5 0	7 0	13 0
Caledonian Brown ,,	—	—	0 4½	—	0 7½	0 10	1 6
Carmine .. .. ,,	0 10½	—	—	1 6	2 9	4 0	7 6
Cerulean Blue .. ,,	0 10½	—	—	1 6	2 9	4 0	7 6
Charcoal Grey .. ,,	—	—	0 4½	—	0 7½	0 10	1 6
Chrome Green Pale ,,	—	0 4½	—	—	0 10½	1 2	2 3
Chrome Green Middle.. ,,	—	0 4½	—	—	0 10½	1 2	2 3
Chrome Green Deep ,,	—	0 4½	—	—	0 10½	1 2	2 3
Chrome Orange ,,	—	0 4½	—	—	0 10½	1 2	2 3
Chrome Yellow Pale ,,	—	0 4½	—	—	0 10½	1 2	2 3
Chrome Yellow Middle ,,	—	0 4½	—	—	0 10½	1 2	2 3
Chrome Yellow Deep ,,	—	0 4½	—	—	0 10½	1 2	2 3
Chromium Oxide Green .. ,,	0 6	—	—	0 10	1 6	2 0	3 6
Cinnabar Green Pale ,,	—	0 4½	—	—	0 10½	1 2	2 3
Cinnabar Green Middle .. ,,	—	0 4½	—	—	0 10½	1 2	2 3
Cinnabar Green Deep .. ,,	—	0 4½	—	—	0 10½	1 2	2 3
Citron Yellow .. ,,	0 6	—	—	0 10	1 6	2 0	3 6

REEVES' ARTISTS' OIL COLOURS—*contd.*

Size of Tube No. ..		2	3	4	4A	8	12	24
		s. d.	s. d.	s. d.	s. d.	s. d.	s. d.	s. d.
obalt Blue ..	EACH	0 10½	—	—	1 6	2 9	4 0	7 6
obalt Green Pale	,,	1 6	—	—	2 9	5 0	7 0	13 0
obalt Green Deep	,,	1 6	—	—	2 9	5 0	7 0	13 0
olbat Violet ..	,,	1 6	—	—	2 9	5 0	7 0	13 0
rimson Lake ..	,,	0 4½	—	—	0 7½	1 0	1 4	2 6
merald Green ..	,,	—	—	0 4½	—	0 10½	1 2	2 3
rench Ultramarine	,,	0 4½	—	—	0 7½	1 0	1 4	2 6
lake White ..	,,	—	—	0 4½	—	0 7½	0 10	1 6
oundation White	,,	—	—	—	—	0 5	0 7½	1 0
amboge Tint ..	,,	0 4½	—	—	0 7½	1 0	1 4	2 6
ndian Red ..	,,	—	—	0 4½	—	0 7½	0 10	1 6
ndian Yellow ..	,,	0 10½	—	—	1 6	2 9	4 0	7 6
ndigo	,,	0 6	—	—	0 10	1 6	2 0	3 6
vory Black ..	,,	—	—	0 4½	—	0 7½	0 10	1 6
talian Lake ..	,,	0 4½	—	—	0 7½	1 0	1 4	2 6
amp Black ..	,,	—	—	0 4½	—	0 7½	0 10	1 6
emon Yellow Pale	,,	0 6	—	—	0 10	1 6	2 0	3 6
emon Yellow Deep	,,	0 6	—	—	0 10	1 6	2 0	3 6
ight Red ..	,,	—	—	0 4½	—	0 7½	0 10	1 6
ars Brown ..	,,	—	—	0 4½	—	0 7½	0 10	1 6
ars Orange ..	,,	—	—	0 4½	—	0 7½	0 10	1 6
ars Violet ..	,,	0 4½	—	—	0 7½	1 0	1 4	2 6
ars Yellow ..	,,	—	—	0 4½	—	0 7½	0 10	1 6
auve—(Aniline)	,,	0 6	—	—	0 10	1 6	2 0	3 6
edium	,,	—	—	0 4½	—	0 7½	0 10	1 6
egilp	,,	—	—	0 4½	—	0 7½	0 10	1 6
aples Red ..	,,	0 6	—	—	0 10	1 6	2 0	3 6
aples Yellow Pale	,,	—	0 4½	—	—	0 10½	1 2	2 3
aples Yellow Deep	,,	—	0 4½	—	—	0 10½	1 2	2 3
eutral Tint ..	,,	—	0 4½	—	—	0 10½	1 2	2 3
ew Blue ..	,,	0 4½	—	—	0 7½	1 0	1 4	2 6
live Green ..	,,	0 4½	—	—	0 7½	1 0	1 4	2 6
ayne's Grey ..	,,	—	0 4½	—	—	0 10½	1 2	2 3
ermanent Blue ..	,,	0 4½	—	—	0 7½	1 0	1 4	2 6
ink Madder ..	,,	0 10½	—	—	1 6	2 9	4 0	7 6
russian Blue ..	,,	—	—	0 4½	—	0 7½	0 10	1 6
aw Sienna ..	,,	—	—	0 4½	—	0 7½	0 10	1 6
aw Umber ..	,,	—	—	0 4½	—	0 7½	0 10	1 6
oman Ochre ..	,,	—	—	0 4½	—	0 7½	0 10	1 6
ose Dore ..	,,	0 10½	—	—	1 6	2 9	4 0	7 6
ose Madder ..	,,	0 10½	—	—	1 6	2 9	4 0	7 6
ose Madder Deep	,,	0 10½	—	—	1 6	2 9	4 0	7 6
ap Green ..	,,	0 4½	—	—	0 7½	1 0	1 4	2 6
carlet Lake ..	,,	0 6	—	—	0 10	1 6	2 0	3 6
ugar of Lead ..	,,	—	—	0 4½	—	0 7½	0 10	1 6
ulphogen Flake White ..	,,	—	—	0 4	—	0 6	0 8	1 2
erre Verte ..	,,	—	—	0 4½	—	0 7½	0 10	1 6
ransparent Golden Ochre ..	,,	—	—	0 4½	—	0 7½	0 10	1 6
ltramarine Ash ..	,,	1 6	—	—	2 9	5 0	7 0	13 0
andyke Brown ..	,,	—	—	0 4½	—	0 7½	0 10	1 6
enetian Red ..	,,	—	—	0 4½	—	0 7½	0 10	1 6
ermilion Pale ..	,,	0 10½	—	—	1 6	2 9	4 0	7 6
ermilion Middle ..	,,	0 10½	—	—	1 6	2 9	4 0	7 6
ermilion Deep ..	,,	0 10½	—	—	1 6	2 9	4 0	7 6
erona Brown ..	,,	—	—	0 4½	—	0 7½	0 10	1 6
iridian	,,	0 10½	—	—	1 6	2 9	4 0	7 6
ellow Ochre ..	,,	—	—	0 4½	—	0 7½	0 10	1 6
inc White ..	,,	—	0 4½	—	—	0 10½	1 2	2 3

THE "LAWRENCE PHILLIPS" PALETTE.
(PATENT.)

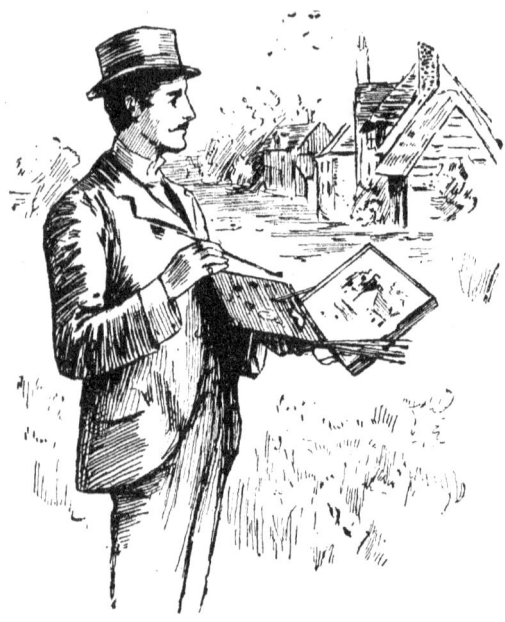

The "Lawrence Phillips" palette to a certain extent may be made to take the place of a sketching box. It consists of a walnut wood palette to which is hinged a panel carrier containing 2 white wood panels.

The panel carrier can be fixed at any suitable angle and is attached to the palette by means of a sliding hinge, so that the painter's coat sleeve does not come into contact with the wet paint. The appliance may be carried about with the palette **wet.**

P. H. CALDERON, R.A., writes :—
"The sliding hinge is a most ingenious arrangement, placing the colours well out of the way of the coat sleeve."

SIR DAVID MURRAY, R.A., writes :—
"I consider it the most serviceable of all handy sketching appliances I have seen."

SIR ALFRED EAST, R.A., writes .—
"Without doubt is the handiest invention for the sketcher in oil I have seen."

STANHOPE FORBES, R.A., writes :—
"It appears to me most admirably contrived."

---

		s.	d.
No. 1	"LAWRENCE PHILLIPS" PALETTE, with 2 panels, 11½ by 8 in..	24	6
	Panels, 11½ by 8 in. . . . . per dozen	9	9
No. 2	"LAWRENCE PHILLIPS" PALETTE, with 2 panels, 8½ by 5 in.	15	6
	Panels, 8½ by 5 in. . . . . per dozen	4	6

REEVES' TEMPERA COLOURS IN TUBES.

NAMES OF COLOURS.

ZINC WHITE	TUBES No. 2 .. EACH	s. d. 0 5
	,, ,, 12 .. ,,	1 10

Burnt Sienna	Raw Umber	
Burnt Umber	Roman Ochre	
Indian Red	Terre Verte	SERIES A.
Ivory Black	Vandyke Brown	s. d. TUBES No. 2 .. EACH 0 5
Lamp Black	Venetian Red	,, ,, 12 .. ,, 1 10
Light Red	Yellow Ochre	
Raw Sienna		

Antwerp Blue		
Indigo		SERIES B.
Naples Yellow Pale		s. d. TUBES No. 2 .. EACH 0 6
Naples Yellow Deep		,, ,, 12 .. ,, 2 3
Prussian Blue		

Alizarin Brn. Madder	Alizarin Scarlet Madder	
Alizarin Crimson	Alizarin Yellow	
Alizarin Green Pale	Crimson Lake	SERIES C.
Alizarin Green Mid.	French Ultramarine	s. d. TUBES No. 2 .. EACH 0 9
Alizarin Green Deep	New Blue	,, ,, 12 .. ,, 3 4
Alizarin Purple Madder	Permanent Blue	

Carmine	Vermilion Pale	SERIES D.
Chromium Oxide Grn.	Vermilion Mid.	s. d. TUBES No. 2 .. EACH 1 0
Lemon Yellow Pale	Vermilion Deep	,, ,, 12 .. ,, 4 6
Lemon Yellow Deep	Viridian	

Cadmium Ex. Pale	Cadmium Deep	SERIES E.
Cadmium Pale	Cobalt Blue	s. d. TUBES No. 2 .. EACH 1 3
Cadmium Mid.	Rose Madder Deep	,, ,, 12 .. ,, 5 8

WALNUT WOOD BOXES FOR OIL PAINTING.

WITHOUT PANELS IN LID.

No. 351.
SKETCHING BOX.

Fitted with 20 tubes of **Artists'** oil colours, large bottles of linseed oil and turpentine, hog hair and fitch brushes, covered dipper, palette knife, and palette.

	s.	d.
Complete .	35	0
Empty with palette .	16	6

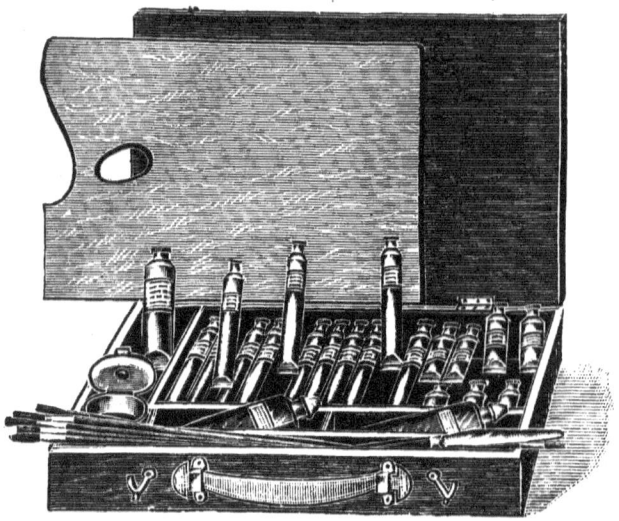

351   (13½ by 9 inches.)

For other sizes see Reeves' Price List.

WOOD OIL SKETCHING BOXES.

MATT POLISH FINISH.

These boxes have an adjustable lid containing two panels which can be raised or lowered by means of a ratchet and rack; the panels can be used horizontally or vertically. The bottom of the box is fitted with three tin trays for colours and brushes, one double tin dipper, two tin oil bottles, and a palette. There is a leather handle and lock and key.

				s.	d.
No. 370	To take panels size 14 in. by 10 in.	each	52	0
No. 371	To take panels size 15 in. by 11 in.	each	55	0
No. 372	To take panels size 16 in. by 12 in.	each	59	6

JAPANNED TIN SKETCHING BOXES

BEST QUALITY BOX.

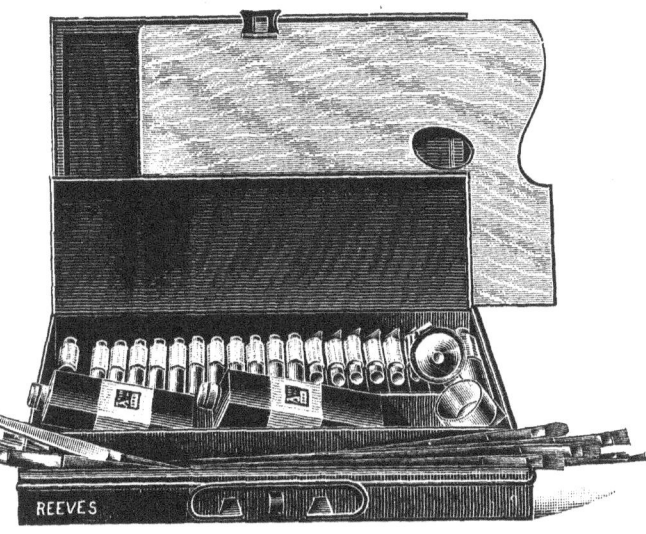

No. 323.
SKETCHING BOX.

Containing palette, hog hair and fitch hair brushes, japanned bottles of oil and turps, palette knife, dipper, and 20 tubes of **Artists'** oil colours.

	s.	d.
Complete .	36	0

323.
(13 × 8½ inches.)

CHEAPER MAKE OF BOX.

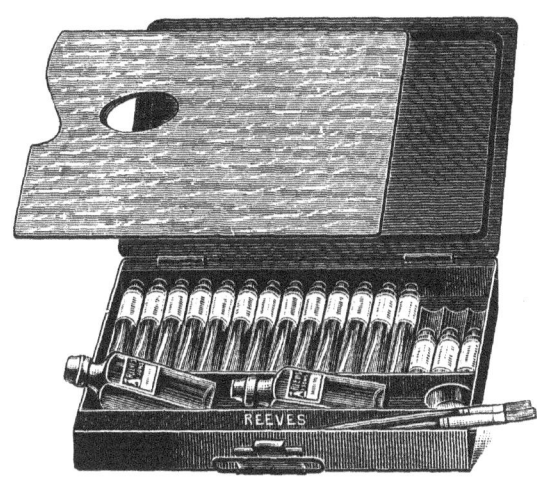

No. 313. SKETCHING BOX

Fitted with **Artists'** oil colours and brushes.

	s.	d.
Complete . . .	13	9

313.
(9½ × 6¾ inches.)

For other sizes see Reeves' Price Lists

www.ingramcontent.com/pod-product-compliance
Lightning Source LLC
Chambersburg PA
CBHW020917180526
45163CB00007B/2771